W9-AXV-832

Fall, 2011
Text Analysis
HCC

Backwards and Forwards

A Technical Manual for Reading Plays

David Ball

Southern Illinois University Press
Carbondale and Edwardsville

for Arthur Ballet and Michael Langham

Library of Congress Cataloging in Publication Data

Ball, David, 1942–
    Backwards and Forwards.

    1. Drama—Technique.   2. Reading comprehension.
I. Title.
PN1661. B34   1983   808.2   82–19333
ISBN 0–8093–1110–0

12 11 10 09   21 20 19 18

Contents

Foreword

Most of us who read playscripts try to imagine them being enacted on a stage. But not all of us, as I discovered when I had the privilege of working for Sir Barry Jackson at the Birmingham Repertory Theatre in England. He was perhaps the last of the great patrons of the British theatre, besides being a man of some eccentricity. Well, when he saw a play on the stage he would try to imagine it back in the book.

Recently I had the opportunity of putting this somewhat bizarre approach to the test. I had been asked to advise about a production of Noel Coward's *Blithe Spirit* which was already on a stage and playing to audiences. I did not read the script, but sat through three performances trying hard to perceive those intentions of the author which had been lost or smudged by the production; i.e., I tried to get back to the original script. I was amazed to discover that Sir Barry's method of comprehending a playwright's meaning is far more immediately effective than the normal method to which David Ball addresses himself in this very helpful book. But Sir Barry's method requires a play on stage.

The usefulness of *Backwards and Forwards* lies in the fact that it reveals a script not only as literature, but as raw material for theatrical performance—sometimes with structural characteristics that make it comparable to a musical score. There is all the difference in the world between literature and drama. A play's sound, music, movement, looks, dynamics—and much more—are to be discovered deep in the script, yet cannot be detected through strictly literary methods of reading and analysis. Looking through this little book is like looking through the playwright's toolbox to discover the special instruments of his craft. For the beginning play-reader *Backwards and Forwards* offers methods that will stretch to incorporate almost everything useful about reading plays. For the reader of more experience—even a lot of experience—there is guidance and illumination about the nature of scripts that can make future expeditions of this kind both richer and more personal.

MICHAEL LANGHAM
The Juilliard School
New York City
1982

Then the King's countenance was
changed, and his thoughts troubled
him so that the joints of his loins were
loosed and his knees smote one
against the other. And the King
spake, and said, "Whosoever shall
read this writing and show me the interpretation thereof, shall be clothed
with scarlet and have a chain of gold
around his neck."

Dan. 5:7

Polonius: What do you read, my lord?
Hamlet: Words. Words. Words.
Polonius: What is the matter, my
            lord?
Hamlet: Between who?
Polonius: I mean the matter that you
            read, my lord.
Hamlet: Slanders, sir . . . for you
            yourself, sir, shall grow old
            as I am if like a crab you
            could go backward.
*Polonius (aside):*Though this be mad-
            ness, yet there is method in't.

Introduction

This book is for people who put plays on the stage: actors, directors, designers, technicians, and playwrights. (It is also for people who read plays just for the sake of reading them—if they agree that the purpose of a script is for it to be staged—but it is addressed directly to those putting plays on the stage. The rest of you may eavesdrop.) A script is not a prose narrative in mere dialogue form. It is writing heavily dependent on special methods and techniques for the stage.

The techniques in this book will help you read analytically to discern how the play *works*. What the play means should not be the first consideration. For the theater artist or technician it is more important to know what makes the clock tick than what time it is. And you can't begin to find a play's meaning until you comprehend its works.

To do your part in staging a script, begin by understanding its mechanics and values. If they are not clear to you, you can't make them clear to an audience so all your best efforts will be wasted. Theater is a combination of artists and technicians, and a script. You can't effectively combine with something you don't understand.

But students of the theater have stopped reading plays. They continue to look at them, sometimes even look at them on the page, but few have the smallest idea why. So

3

actors, despite talent and sophisticated training, can't. Designers get notions, not concepts. Playwrights with no idea why the ghost of Hamlet's father does not talk until scene 5 or what it talks about type decades of trivia. And directors *block*, nothing more.

The theater artist who perceives little on the page puts little on the stage. So there are legions of would-be's whose careers never gain the name of action. From nothing, after all, comes nothing.

This book is about techniques of reading scripts. Technique is not always in favor among students. But just as inspired acting, design, and directing depend on technical mastery, so does intelligent and imaginative script reading. Inspiration without technique—if it exists at all—is merely flair. If inspiration is all you have it will abandon you when you need it most.

This book describes only technique. You must provide inspiration, intelligence, imagination. They cannot be taught or written about. They can barely be described. But technique will make their appearance more likely, and will get you through those unavoidable, frequent times when inspiration, intelligence, and imagination don't appear.

Technique, like any good tool, will not limit your result. There is no single "correct" interpretation of any good play, but sound reading techniques will help ensure that your interpretations are valid and stageworthy.

Analyzing the script is a lot of work—at least as much work as whatever else you do in theater. But if you have the technique and diligence to read scripts properly, your market value will have a competitive chance. If an actor, you'll leap casting couches in a single bound. If a designer, you'll design, not decorate plays. If a director, you'll *be* a director—not an assistant stage manager—and you'll be hired by producers aware of your value from the first interview. And if a playwright, you might discover how to make a script for an audience beyond your English class.

William Shakespeare's *Hamlet* is referred to over and over in this book. Read *Hamlet*, and have it at hand when reading *Backwards and Forwards*. Several other plays are referred to; if you don't know them well, treat each first mention as a reading assignment. Don't cheat yourself by skipping or skimming. Too many people will always be after your theater job (if you ever get one) for you to survive being lazy.

Once you have mastered reading techniques, no script can intimidate you. And you will find skilled script reading a special pleasure. Skilled reading is nothing like the drudgery of dumb reading. Unfortunately, it is also not as widespread.

A Word about Terms

Climax, point of attack, denouement, rising action, falling action, spine, and Aristotle's *plot, character* and *thought,* along with a myriad of other terms, reflect a myriad of approaches to scripts. There is little agreement about precise meaning of such terms, and less agreement about how to apply them to play analysis. This does not invalidate them, but we must be wary. For example, does climax mean the point of highest emotional involvement? Whose emotional involvement: the audience's or the characters' in the play? Or does it mean something else altogether: the point where the action reverses direction? The two are not always in the same place. A discussion of climax without first defining our particular use of the word will be confusing and misleading. Even once climax is defined, you have to know how to find it—and that is where you need more specific analytical tools.

It is easy to say, with Aristotle, that a play's main ingredients are plot, character, and thought. But they are results, not first steps. They are what you have to find, *not how you have to find them.* This book is about *how.*

A play's plot is the product of other elements. Character—particularly in drama—is not where analysis starts, but where it ends. On stage (or in real life) character is amorphous, shifting, intangible. Understanding character requires analysis of its components—concrete, palpable components.

And *thought:* don't even think about a play's thought until you understand the concrete elements of which the play is composed. This book is about concrete elements.

Plot, character, thought—and the rest—are terms useful in describing some of the results of careful analysis. But they do not often provide the best means to get there.

Because each reader must etch out particular definitions of existing terms, because most terms describe results not methods, and because many terms describe the vague and amorphous, this book uses terms in carefully defined ways. By understanding terms *as used in this book* you will be half way to understanding the methods they comprise.

Script analysis is an exacting craft. Its terms are your tools, and you want to be clear on the precise nature of your tools. If you can't distinguish a hammer from an ax, you won't build much of a house. Nor will you chop down much of a tree.

Part One

Shape

1

What Happens That Makes Something Else Happen?

First, good Peter Quince, say what the
play treats on. . . .
A Midsummer Night's Dream 1.2.8

A play is a series of *actions.* A play is not *about* action, nor
does it *describe* action. Is a fire about flames? Does it describe flames? No, a fire *is* flames. A play *is* action.

Why do you think actors are called *actors?*

Then what is action? For script analysis, action is a very
particular entity. **Action occurs when something happens
that makes or permits something else to happen.** Action is
two "something happenings," *one leading to the other.* Something causes or permits something else. I let go of my pen-
cil (half an action); it falls to the floor (the other half of the
action). Together those two connected events make an action.

If I say "How are you?" it is half an action. The second
half is your saying, "Fine, thank you." The first leads to the
second; the two compose an action.

The gasoline in a Mercedes is not action, nor is the car's
nature (its character): shape, mechanical configuration,
specifications, color, seat covers of snail-darter hide. A
Mercedes has to do with action only when it progresses—
only when it goes from one place to another.

So the first thing to discover is how a play goes from one
place to another. Find the first *event* of each action, then
the second, then the connection between the two. The

9

play's journey is contained within its actions, and getting there is half the fun. A fine play gets us there first class, complimentary champagne, exquisite companionship, memorable service. A bad play is a Calcutta bus. But for both we must know every connection between every event, from the start of the play onwards (or, as we shall see, just the other way around).

Try it. Look at any scene in *Hamlet*. Find out its journey. *What happens that makes something else happen?* To begin with, worry about nothing else.

What happens that leads to something else happening? If you can answer that for every event in *Hamlet*, you will know more about the play than years of seminars and shelves of books can reveal. And you will begin to master the play for yourself, in your own terms. This is essential if you intend to do anything with the play other than muse over it.

If I (1) walk into your room shouting that the building is on fire and you (2) flee for your life, that is action.

If you (1) flee for your life leaving me free to (2) steal your stamp collection, that is another action.

If I (1) steal your stamp collection and then (2) sell it, that is yet another action.

Stealing your stamp collection is not an action until I sell it. One event requires a second event, connected. How else can it be part of a play's progression?

An event without a second, connected event, without effect or result, is either inadequate playwriting or, more likely, inadequate play reading. In life and on stage unconnected events are irrelevant. Life aside, it is hard to make irrelevance theatrically viable.

If I do anything that leads you to do anything, together we have an action. If I fire a gun at you and you fall over in a dead heap, we have an action. Your first task when reading a play is to find each action: find each action's first event (its *trigger*), then its second event (its *heap*). Both will be there. There is a heap for every trigger and vice-versa.

Instant-by-instant, moment-by-moment, from start to

finish, the playwright crafts a *series* of actions: trigger and heap, trigger and heap. Find them all.

FOCUS: *An event is anything that happens. When one event causes or permits another event, the two events together comprise an action. Actions are a play's primary building blocks.*

2

And What Happens Next?

And it must follow as the night the
day. . . .

Hamlet 1.3.79

Each trigger leads to a new heap. (Each event causes or
permits a second event.) That is one action. But now the
heap, the second event, becomes a trigger: a new *first* event
of a new action.

A first event: the ghost of Hamlet's father tells its grisly
tale (1. 5). The second event: Hamlet vows to devote himself
to revenge. Read the scene to discover the connection between the two events. Then see how the second event becomes the *next* action's first event (how heap becomes trigger). Hamlet's vow of revenge leads to a new heap: he
swears his comrades to secrecy.

What is the next action? First event: Hamlet swears his
comrades to secrecy. Second event (the next thing Hamlet
does): he acts strangely towards Ophelia. If you discover
how this action's second event (heap) becomes the next action's first event (trigger)—that is, if you discover what
Hamlet can do as a result of his strange behavior towards
Ophelia—you will be on your way to the core of the script.
You still have vast leeway for your own interpretations, but
you won't wander from the play.

If you can discover such connections between events, you
will be able to take us, step by step, event by connected
event, action by action, right to the heap of bodies at play's
end. But if you can't, then no matter how much you under-

stand character or meaning or Freud or world views or philosophy, you can't stage the play. Unfortunately, that rarely
stops anyone from trying.

Try an experiment: stand a domino on end. Stand
another domino next to it. Push the first domino over, and
it will, if cleverly arranged, knock down the second.

A play is like a series of dominoes: one event triggers the
next, and so on. At first, reading a play this way is difficult,
like learning to drive a standard shift car. But learning to
get out of first gear is never easy. Only practice teaches any
technique worth having. Don't cheat the talent you believe
you have by skipping this first step. It is the foundation.

Consider the dominoes. I rush into your room hollering
fire. You flee in panic. I take your stamp collection. I sell
the collection at the pawnshop for cash. I give the cash to
the doctor for my baby's operation. The doctor operates . . .
and on and on until the heap of corpses or the wedding in
the last act.

Sometimes the domino path divides to become multiple.
(A trigger leads to two or more simultaneous heaps.) There
is no need for confusion if you examine the separate paths
domino by domino, spotting the connection between each
adjacent domino. Analyzed this way, no complication of
plot will defeat you.

The key is *adjacent* dominoes: the collision of each
domino into the one right next to it. Never skip a step. If
you cannot find the connection between one domino and
the next (why or how one makes the next fall), then there is
a problem either in the writing or in your reading. Either is
possible, but at least the problem will be located. That is
the first step to solving it.

Sequential, domino-by-domino analysis will help you
avoid misleading choices about the play. For example, generations of well-meaning commentators claim Hamlet is
incapable of action. Yet examination of even the first two
acts domino by domino reveals Hamlet initiating more
direct action than most people manage in a year. How in-
sulting to the Bard are these commentators! Could Shake-

speare have wanted his audience to spend hours watching a character do nothing? For that is what someone incapable of action does: nothing.

If only those commentators knew what you know now, they would see that Hamlet does almost everything *but* nothing. Sequential analysis of action is the door to the play and protection against misinterpretation.

FOCUS: *An action is comprised of two events: a trigger and a heap. Each heap becomes the next action's trigger, so that actions are like dominoes toppling one into the next. Sequential analysis means following the play domino by domino from start to finish.*

3

But Do It Backwards

Come, come, you froward and unable worms. . . .

The Taming of the Shrew 5.2.169

I can walk into your room, but I don't *have* to yell fire. I can
stab myself instead, or stub my toe, or read a book, or
compliment you on your shoes. That is what free will is all
about. Even if I yell fire, nothing predetermines that you
flee the room. You may instead throw your stamps out the
window to save them, then call the fire brigade.

An examination of dominoes only as they move *forward*
through a play leaves everything arbitrary. You (1) walk
into a bookstore, (2) find the drama shelf, (3) take down this
book, (4) pay for it, and (5) leave. But you could have (1)
walked into a bookstore and (2) found the candy counter.
Or you might have (2) seen the place full of books and (3)
fled in chagrin. Even had you picked up this book, instead
of paying for it you might have slipped it under your ethics
text and sneaked out. And you might have got away with it,
or you might have not. Life goes *on;* it goes *forward*—but
never predictably.

Only when we look at events in reverse order can we see,
with certainty, how the dominoes fell, which fell against
which. The fact that you (4) stand at the cash register paying for this book requires that you (3) found the book.

Going forwards allows unpredictable possibility.

Going backwards exposes that which is required.

15

The present demands and reveals a specific past. One particular, identifiable event lies immediately before any other. But who can say what comes next? It can be anything. The next thing you see may be the next paragraph or it may be a little man from Mars. You don't know for sure until you can look back on it.

Examining events backwards ensures you will have no gaps in your comprehension of the script. When you discover an event you cannot connect to a previous event, you know there is a problem for either reader or writer to solve.

Examine the events in *Hamlet* in reverse order. Don't complain that it's difficult or time-consuming; if doing theater were easy there would be nothing striking about succeeding at it.

Begin at the end of act 5. Where did this heap of bodies come from? Let's look at one, for example, the one with the crown askew and the stab wound. He must have been the king. Claudius is dead, a felled domino. What felled it? Not "What might have felled it all along," but "What felled it *right now?*" What was adjacent? Was it not Hamlet? But what had *just* happened to Hamlet?

Lots of things had happened to Hamlet but only one thing had *just* happened. Among the lots of things, for instance: a ghost had talked to Hamlet, but that was a few acts ago. And Hamlet had fought with pirates (not bad for a man incapable of action), but that's long past, too. Neither pirates nor ghost was the domino that felled Hamlet into felling the king. *A domino can fell only the domino next to it, no other*—just like real dominoes.

Look for the adjacent domino. Skip nothing.

What is the adjacent domino immediately before Hamlet stabs Claudius? Is it in Laertes' speech?

Hamlet, thou art slain.
No med'cine in the world can do thee good;
In thee there is not half an hour's life.

[5.2.313–15]

What an astonishingly clear play! How can it puzzle anyone? What need of convoluted investigation or philosophy? In less than twenty-five words Hamlet is told three unambiguous times he's about to die. But this is not quite the adjacent domino; it's too far back from the stabbing of Claudius. If the trigger domino were Hamlet finding out he was about to die, he would stab Claudius right then. But he doesn't; he has not yet the cue for action. Fortunately Laertes continues:

> The treacherous instrument is in thy hand,
> Unbated and envenomed. The foul practise
> Hath turned itself on me. Lo, here I lie
> Never to rise again.

[316–19]

No one needs a footnote to understand that Laertes too is dying. But still Hamlet does not kill Claudius. We still lack the domino that turns Hamlet into regicide and avenger. Laertes continues to speak, but still no domino sways. Suspense builds: will the domino never fall?

> Thy mother's poisoned.
> I can no more.

[319–20]

Now every groundling knows that if Laertes says no more there will be no more dominoes—hence no heap. But now comes the domino. It is nothing subtle. Shakespeare, as always, hands it to us, explodes it for us. Laertes says,

> The King! The King's to blame!

[320]

At that instant, not before, Hamlet does what he has been on the verge of doing all along: he kills the king. The killing awaited the right domino, and that domino could not fall until some preceding right domino fell first. And so on all the way *back* to the beginning. Moving backwards from the heap of bodies, we find the precipitating domino with ease.

Try it. What domino falls that makes Laertes speak the speech quoted above ("Hamlet, thou art slain")? Is it the fact he is mortally wounded? And what falling domino mortally wounded him? You can begin acting, directing, or designing Laertes only if you have traced his dominoes back to his first involvement in the play. And until you can do that for Hamlet, you haven't read the play that is worth reading.

There is little in *Hamlet* that a normal fifteen-year-old cannot fathom. Prove it. Tread where wise men have trod with caution: investigate Hamlet himself. Work backwards on him, domino by domino, cue by cue, action by action, precipitous event by precipitous event. End with the true beginning of his action: the Ghost impelling him to revenge (1.5).

The complexity and depth of the play can unfold itself to you without footnotes, without confusion. You can comfortably understand every unit part of the play via the clear, simple steps Shakespeare provided.

But remember: make no large jumps. Find the preceding *adjacent* domino. Don't miss links. Hamlet does not kill Claudius because the Ghost talked to Hamlet in act 1, scene 5. Hamlet kills Claudius because of what Laertes says the instant before the killing. Of such adjacent links is life— and drama—made up.

FOCUS: *Sequential analysis of actions is most useful when done backwards: from the end of the play back to the start. It is your best insurance that you understand why everything happens.*

4
Stasis and Intrusion

I will not stir from this place, do what
they can!
A Midsummer Night's Dream 3.1.121-22

Stasis is motionlessness: a condition of balance among various forces; a standing still; an *unchanging* stability; a state in which all forces balance each other, resulting in no movement.

Intrusion is a pushing, thrusting, or forcing in.

In a script's structure, dominoes are atoms. Now let us step back to expand our view from atoms to planets.

The course of a play charts the movement of a world. The world may be a royal castle in Denmark, or the top of a rubbish heap, or Scotland in turmoil, or England divided in three, or George and Martha's living room in a small college town, or Thebes ravaged by plague.

First the playwright presents the world in *stasis*.

Hamlet presents Denmark, a long time ago, at the palace of the king. There's a prince named Hamlet. He's unhappy because his father recently died and his mother married again, rather soon. That is the static situation. Nothing is changing. The balance of all the forces involved has produced a complacent new ruler, a melancholy prince, a worried mother. None of them has sufficient reason to try to change anything. It is absolute stasis—but something awaits.

19

Oedipus Tyrannos presents Thebes, in Greece, a long time ago, outside the palace of the king. The king is inside, presumably asleep with his wife. Outside the populace suffers through a plague. That is the static situation. Until the plague turns so unbearable that it impels the populace to wail for help, this world too is motionless: without motive, reason or cue for change. It is absolute stasis.

Macbeth presents Scotland, a long time ago, where a noble and loyal thane has bravely served his king in battle and is on his way to be praised and rewarded. His sense of ambition is held respectably in check (i.e., *balanced*) by his loyalty to crown and law. We are in the midst of safe, prudent stasis.

King Lear presents England, a long time ago, at the king's castle. The aged king, ready to retire, has arranged to cast off his burdens by dividing his realm among his three daughters. A public ceremony is in preparation for the king to demonstrate that his three daughters are overwhelmingly devoted to him. That is the static situation. Barring the unexpected, this will remain a predictable, *unchanging* situation: stasis.

When Lear's daughter Cordelia is asked what she has to say to show how much she loves her father, she responds, "Nothing, my lord" (1.1.87). Stasis is broken. Lear is first puzzled, then hurt, then enraged; by the time of his rage the play is well in motion.

You sit in your room, reading. You glance from time to time at your treasured stamp collection, secure in the knowledge it is safe from me because you are there to guard it. This is stasis.

The world presented at play's beginning is in stasis. Occasionally stasis is broken before the play starts, but even then we know what stasis was. We understand what life was like in Salem before the first reports of witches. If we didn't, the witches would seem no intrusion. *And for a play to begin to play, there must be an intrusion.*

In every play something or someone comes along to shatter stasis. A ghost says your father was foully murdered by your Uncle Claudius, now king. A populace howls from the palace steps for you to make the plague in Thebes go away. Three witches dance gibbering around a cauldron and call you Thane of Cawdor and, hail to thee, Macbeth, king hereafter. Your favorite daughter, Cordelia, will not gush about how much more she loves you than do her hypocritical sisters (who have just sworn wordy oaths that they love you more than words can wield the matter). Someone barges into your room where you sit reading and contemplating stamps; he cries, "Fire!"

In every case that intrusion is the starting bell. We are off! The world of stasis—unmoving, unchanging, unstriving—is jarred into action.

You sit safely in your backyard licking stamps: stasis. Suddenly a great bird swoops down, talons you, and flies you off beyond the horizon to drop you into the ocean. You swim for dear life, reach shore, hitch a ride back to town, then . . . you manage any series of events until finally you are home again, stamps retrieved from the fiend who sent the bird. You erect an overhead fence to keep birds out. *Stasis is reestablished.* This is the goal in every play, whether this reestablished stasis is the same as the original stasis, or a new one. *Stasis comes about at the close of the play when the major forces of the play either get what they want or are forced to stop trying.*

Hamlet, once he has heard the Ghost, is not interested in returning to his original stasis (actionless depression). It is a grave misreading to say the play is about a man depressed. Only the beginning stasis is about depression. *Intrusion usually changes everything that can be changed.* In *Hamlet,* after the Ghost's speech of act 1, scene 5, hardly a line in the play hints that Hamlet is depressed. Yet generations of commentators have seen the entire play in the light of its initial stasis, and have developed whole interpretations grounded in depression ("melancholia"). If only they understood dramatic structure! The Ghost (*intrusion*) catapults Hamlet headlong into action, into battle, at a breathtaking pace that leaves no room for sluggish depression. An evening of depressed Hamlet is as untheatrical as an evening of actionless Hamlet, and as depressing.

For every play, scrutinize the *difference* between the world in stasis and the world in action. This difference will illuminate the forces that drive the play and ensure that you avoid depression.

First comes stasis, then intrusion—and then all the resources of the play's world swing into gear. High-energy forces battle each other until a new stasis comes about.

Intrusion upon stasis is an event (see section 1, above), an event that causes another event—hence: action. A character or characters try to right things. You (2) rush out of the room to save yourself after I've (1) yelled "fire." Lear, trying to establish new stasis, banishes the recalcitrant Cordelia and divides his kingdom between Goneril and Regan so he might, he hopes, yet live happily ever after.

If you or Lear succeed in your first response to the intrusion, the play ends. But I steal your stamps, and Goneril and Regan have other plans for Lear. So you and Lear have to try again, and the play continues, domino to domino, until the characters finally succeed, or can no longer try, or are defeated. Then the play ends.

Sometimes a new stasis is not what the character hoped it would be, so the play does not end. Macbeth is catapulted into action by the witches; he strives for a new stasis he thinks will satisfy him: gaining the crown. But that turns out to be no stasis after all; he must go beyond it. The forces at work must change direction, seek new stasis—and the play continues.

 Remember the steps: stasis, intrusion, and the battle for new stasis initiated by intrusion.

Ferret out the moment of intrusion and from it carefully follow the dominoes. Know the forces, the energies, the central moves that the intrusion unleashes to catapult the play into action. Know the *goals* of the battle: the new stasis being sought.

These steps will spare your audiences four hours of depressed Danish prince or two hours of incomprehensible Scottish thane drooling with ambition long after there's nothing left to drool for.

Dramatic stasis occurs when things would go on the same forever if something didn't come along and happen. Dramatic intrusion is the thing that comes along and happens, setting free the irresistible forces that run a play from that point on. As you begin to perceive of Hamlet (like Lear, like Oedipus, like Hedda, like Willy Loman, like Romeo, like you in the ocean, like Macbeth) as driven by irresistible forces, you may be surprised that in the middle of act 3 he seems depressed again and talks of killing himself. You may be too surprised to believe that "To be or not to be" (3.1) is a soliloquy about suicide. You may even realize it's no soliloquy. Hamlet knows he has listeners: Polonius and the king.

By act 3, scene 1 Hamlet has no reason to consider killing himself, and we know he's no longer depressed. *But* Claudius and Polonius *don't* know that, and Hamlet knows they don't. Hamlet knows they could easily be convinced he has gone over the edge.

Use your domino technique to find why Hamlet would *pretend* to contemplate suicide. As a first step, ask yourself what event causes Hamlet to come to this particular place at this particular time. (It is revealed for all to see, though most don't, in act 3, scene 1, line 29: Claudius says, "We have closely sent for Hamlet hither.") If Hamlet knows he has been sent for, and if he knows Polonius is a master spy (Does he? How does he know it? Where is it revealed?), then indeed this most famous of soliloquies is no soliloquy. It is a maneuver by Hamlet, who knows he is being over-heard by the folks who have sent for him, a maneuver aimed at Claudius to help Hamlet regain stasis in a world that went topsy-turvy in act 1, scene 5 when the Ghost re-vealed how rotten things were in the state of Denmark.

Interpret the maneuver as you will, so long as you don't mistake "To be or not to be" for an action-interrupting di-gression on suicide. Structural investigation of stasis and intrusion shows it is not. Why would Hamlet, generally ac-knowledged to be Shakespeare's most intelligent character, stupidly refer to death as "the undiscovered country from whose bourne no traveller returns"? Can Hamlet have forgotten whom he saw in act 1, scene 5?

Never accept commonplace or even sophisticated assumptions about any play. You are an artist; do your *own* interpretation. That doesn't mean novelty for its own sake, or twisting the work beyond itself. It means mastery of analytic reading techniques to help you to your own conclusions, conclusions that illuminate, not violate, the script.

Examine ten favorite plays. Find initial stasis in each, then intrusion, then discern the forces that drive the play from intrusion to final stasis at play's end.

Plays do not wander. No irresistible forces do. A play's unleashed force is sufficient to drive it through the evening. It won't allow for wandering. *Build your awareness around the rush and collision of conflicting forces.* If you don't, you will slumber the poor folks in the audience whose only error was to trust your ability to interest them.

FOCUS: Stasis *is the status quo that has existed in the play's world up through its beginning.* Intrusion *is something that upsets the status quo, causing or releasing forces that compose the play's conflict and progress. When the forces no longer conflict, new stasis is achieved and the play ends.*

5
Obstacle, Conflict

Fie, Joan, that thou wilt be so obstacle.
Henry VI, Part 1 5.4.17

People who talk about, write about, or do theater agree on
little. But there is one thing: "Drama is *conflict!*" we all cry
in rare unanimity. Then we go back to squabbling over
whether *Measure for Measure* is a comedy.

But what is conflict? The word is used so much that we
rarely scrutinize it for meaning. That leads to sloppy play
analysis. Conflict is central to drama, so we must be clear
what conflict is.

Specifically: what is *dramatic conflict?*

It is not a general crash of one thing into another. It is a
particular kind of interaction, deeply rooted in and in-
alienable from real-life human behavior. The nature of
conflict is so simple that many readers don't notice it, or
they think it is something else.

Historical Origin of Dramatic Conflict, Concise Version

An ancient Greek in a ceremony honoring a recently-
deceased heroic warrior-ruler utters words of praise and
lament in chorus with other ancient Greeks. "Oh ye Gods!"
howls the chorus. "How can we survive without brave Pesticles, he who quelled the hordes from the north, he who
defeated the ravaging ships from the sea, he who . . ." and
on and on till there's not a dry Athenian eye listening. "Oh
Pesticles, son of Panticles, son of Pedicles, son of . . ." the
chant continues.

25

So far there is no dramatic conflict—hence, no drama.
There is no drama even though the chanters chant in
front of an audience, no drama even if they tell a story
("Oh Pesticles, you who mounted your horse one stormy
night and with your mighty sword took the head from the
Mongolian savage"), no drama even if the chanters are
ceremonially dressed, even if a hard-working Athenian has
painted up some backdrops with garlands, pillars, and
leaves. There is no drama even if the chanters bow and re-
ceive applause at the end. *There is no drama because the
elemental ingredient is missing.* Those who call Thespis the
first actor just because he stepped out in front of the chorus
miss the point. Something is still lacking, the crucial event
at the heart of drama that has shaped drama from the
start. Snout, in *A Midsummer Night's Dream,* brings us
closer to this heart of drama:

> In this same interlude it doth befall
> That I, one Snout by name, *present a wall,*
> And such a wall, *as I would have you think,*
> That had in it a crannied hole or chink
> Through which the lovers, Pyramus and Thisbe,
> Did whisper often, very secretly.
> This loam, this rough-cast, and this stone doth show
> That *I am that same wall.* The truth is so.
>
> [5.1.155–62; emphasis added]

Unlike Snout, the ancient Athenian lamenting and prais-
ing dead Pesticles never pretends to be anyone but himself.
The great invention was more than stepping to the front of
the chorus to talk alone. *The great invention was to pretend
to be someone else.* Thespis was no actor until he *pretended
to be Pesticles.* His garb was not theatrical costume until its
purpose was to make the audience think he was Pesticles.
And painted backdrops became "scenery" only when intended to *represent* a place other than the stage, such as the
shore where Pesticles repelled the barbarian invaders.
The actor implicitly makes a request of the audience, and
in that request lies the foundation of drama: "Pretend I am

Pesticles, this chiton his chiton, this chlamys his chlamys, and this place the bloody sands whereon he fought." When Thespis stepped downstage and said, "I am Pesticles," it was a giant step. It was a new step, a clever but difficult step, because pretending to be someone else presents some absolutely inalterable requirements.

The most important requirement is plausibility. You must do as little as possible to remind the audience you are actually *not* the character you represent. When playing a lion, if you let your face show through your mask the audience will be continually reminded you are no lion.

When pretending to be someone else, you must portray believable human behavior. If you do things human beings (or lions, as the case may be) do not do, the audience will not believe your impersonation. Your pretense will fail.

Over the ages there have been variations in the extent actors have tried to be plausible, but even at the low end of the scale *support of the impersonation, support of the pretense*, has been theater's first order of business.

What has this to do with conflict? This: characters in plays *talk* a lot. Talking is drama's most common activity. Talking conveys nearly all we are likely to know about a play, its people, its progress. All this talking, of course, must occur in a way that *supports the pretense of impersonation*. So playwrights try to reflect recognizable human behavior in how their characters talk. Playwrights may heighten language, or lower it, or fragment it, or make it as artificial as can be, but because they want to support, not undermine, the pretense of impersonation, they always try to present talking as recognizable human behavior.

What is it about talking that connects it to recognizable human behavior? *A human being talks in order to get what he or she wants.*

That is the key to dramatic language, a language quite distinct from poetry and nondramatic written prose.

And it is the key to a child learning to talk. Babies learn words as tools to control their environments—*to get what they want.* Perhaps maturity is nothing more than learning

better ways than yowling to get what we want. When the
infant screams and turns red, or when the adult intones, "I
prithee, gentle mortal," both *want* something.

What a character wants motivates talking. A human being
thinks many things never spoken. From the many things
one thinks, one selects what to say according to what one
wants.

Put another way: if you *want* nothing, you *say* nothing.

Not everything in drama mirrors real life, but this does.
A character who speaks wants something or would not
speak. This common element of human nature is the basis
for all drama.

That was a long way around to understand so concise a
fact. The fact's universality is not based on aesthetics but
exists because drama involves impersonation, because impersonation must avoid the blatantly implausible, and because speech devoid of a motivation of wanting is blatantly
implausible.

So the bad playwright sets down, for some poor actor to
recite, exposition like, "You are my brother, as you know."
These are words forced into a character's mouth that have
to do with the *playwright's* want (conveying information to
the audience) instead of the *character's* want.

Whether I want something determines whether I talk.
What I want determines what I say. Playwrights who don't
know this write endless chatter. Actors who don't know it
turn taut drama to chatter. Designers who don't know it
use theater for a place to hang their patterns. Directors
who don't know it should be hung. The gallows would be
filled for a year.

An obstacle is any resistance to my having what I want.
What I want and what resists my having it (*obstacle*) work
against each other to create dramatic conflict.

**Dramatic conflict is distinct from other kinds of conflict.
A novel's conflict might be free will versus destiny. A
poem's conflict might be youth versus old age, or the city
versus the country. But a play's conflict is between what
someone wants and what hinders the want: the obstacle.**

Whether I want something determines whether I talk.

Precisely what I say depends on what I want *and* what is in my way (obstacle). I speak what I consider the most efficient possible words to remove or get around the obstacle.

The baby is thirsty. He wants to drink. Obstacle: the nearest liquid is across the room where he can't get to it. To overcome the obstacle the tyke screeches, "Wawa!" or "Mama!" Thirty years later he is capable of more articulate expression: "Johnny Walker Red on the rocks with a twist." In both cases the obstacle is dealt with by talking.

It is not enough to understand why a character thinks something. You must know *why it is said aloud.* What is wanted (*motivation*)? What is in the way (*obstacle*)?

Obstacles are easily ignored, unfortunately. Actors remember motivations but not obstacles. Yet a motivation not set against the energizing resistance of an obstacle results in words delivered slackly, automatically, slickly. No resistance means no dramatic conflict. That means no play, no matter what else the actor does. The last two minutes of a 95 to 27 basketball game is like a motivation without an obstacle: not worth watching.

Directors also forget obstacles. So whole productions of *Hamlet* exhibit no inkling of why Hamlet doesn't just stab Claudius in act 1, scene 6.

Designers forget not only obstacle but motivation too. So Macbeth's castle is made gloomy, dark, as foreboding as death. Only a submoronic Duncan would enter it, much less compliment how welcoming and pleasant it looks. This kind of error stems from reading for mood and general impression ("atmosphere") rather than specific human behavior.

You do not really know a play until you see how every word is intended by its speaker to overcome some obstacle to what the speaker wants. The issue can be of major import (Lear wanting to give up his kingdom) or trivial, but there is no other reason for a character to talk. This simple principle would by itself edit away half the words from the scripts of many young playwrights. Then someone might stage their plays.

An obstacle can be anything. Often it stems from what

someone else wants. (Motivation: I want to be king. Obstacle: *you* want to *stay* king.) Obstacle can also stem from circumstances, or one's own inabilities or misgivings, or from chance or fate. In every case, the obstacle must be something I am willing to fight. If I am not, I do nothing—so there's no action. So the audience goes to sleep.

I love you (motivation). You think I am a creep (obstacle). So I say something to try changing your attitude ("Care for a ride in my Mercedes?")

You desperately want a job (motivation). The interviewer must select from thirty applicants (obstacle). So you try to impress the interviewer ("I've done this kind of work before").

Jack cannot stand Jill so wants her to go away. Jack's obstacle: Jill will not leave him alone. So Jack says something intended to get rid of her ("Go away," or "I have the measles").

A play gives only result: the words spoken. You must figure out the motivation and obstacle that lead to "Care for a ride in my Mercedes?" or "I have the measles."

Even habitual, trivial actions rest on motivation and obstacle, though it may be harder to find them out. For example, you say good morning to your neighbor. You have said good morning to your neighbor every morning for eight years. Motivation? Obstacle? To find them out, consider the consequences if you *don't* say good morning: your neighbor may think something you do not want him to think. *Even habitual actions* ("Hi," "Nice day," etc.) *must be launched from the attempt to get something you want against something resisting your getting it.*

Dramatic conflict—want versus obstacle—can be of four types. Some or all appear in every play. From the main character's point of view, these types of dramatic conflict are:

1. *Me against myself.* I want your stamp collection, but I know that stealing is wrong and I have difficulty bringing myself to do it. If I want the stamps badly enough I will try to overcome the obstacle (my moral stance against steal-

ing). The conflict is between me and my own reservations: me against myself.

2. *Me against other individuals.* I want your stamps, but you guard them with a baseball bat. This conflict is between me and *you:* me against another individual.

3. *Me against society.* I stole your stamps. Now I am wanted by the F.B.I., hunted like a dog. I broke the law; now society's wrath hounds me. My adversary is not you; I am fighting for my freedom, and I am fighting against society.

4. *Me against fate, or the universe, or natural forces, or God or the gods.* This is a hard battle to win! It is man against the sheer cliff of a mountain, or Lear howling "Blow winds" at the storm, or Macbeth refusing to accept his fate, crying "Lay on, Macduff!" It is not a conflict likely to result from my stealing your stamps.

In all four cases the battle is between what I want and my obstacles. The better the play, the more the force of motivation is irresistible and the more the obstacle is immovable, regardless of the classification of dramatic conflict. But be sure that you know not only what overriding conflict is present in a play, but also which classification is involved at each instant of the play. This will prevent staging *King Lear* or *Oedipus Tyrannos* as family melodrama or social commentary, or *Waiting for Godot* as high tragedy.

Dramatic conflict (motivation versus obstacle) is the force that drives the play from action to action. It makes the difference between theater and recitation.

FOCUS: A character's want is opposed by some hindrance— by some obstacle. A character talks to maneuver another character or characters in such a way that the obstacle to the want is removed. To understand a line of dialogue you must know what the speaker wants and how the speaker intends the words spoken to overcome the obstacle to what is wanted.

6

Ignorance Is Bliss

(Or: The Very Cause of Everyone's Lunacy about *Hamlet*)

Alack, for lesser knowledge!
The Winter's Tale 2.1.38

Point by point through the script, know what information has been revealed, and what has been withheld. In production, do not reveal information prematurely or you might undermine the foundation of the play like high-speed termites. The gap between what the audience knows and doesn't *yet* know can be crucial. Bridge it too early at your peril.

Don't spill the beans too soon!

What could be more obvious? Yet people direct *Hamlet* or write books about it without ever considering at what point the *audience* discovers that Claudius is guilty. So the actor playing Claudius portrays him obviously guilty right from the start. The cat's out of the bag, the audience cheated by knowing too soon.

Read with the naive perspective of a first-time audience, and you cannot know Claudius is guilty until act 3—just one scene before Hamlet himself finds out.

If you know from the start Claudius is guilty, you can't see the mystery-story core of the first three acts. If you can't see the mystery story, you miss what Hamlet is doing (trying to find out whether Claudius is guilty)—so you assume

32

he does nothing. This may be one source of the lunatic view that Hamlet is incapable of action.

But Hamlet works hard, from the Ghost's tale onward, to discover whether the spirit he saw was the devil with false information or a true spirit with facts. If you consider Hamlet's situation, if you consider where power lies in that Danish court, and if you consider the fact that you just can't query someone about whether he or she killed your father (it's a breach of etiquette even in Denmark, and in any case not likely to get a straight answer), you may see why Hamlet begins his maneuvering with a protective mask of madness. It helps him solve the mystery of whether or not Claudius is guilty, and that mystery is the mainspring of the play's first half. Hamlet wants to solve it *and the audience does too.* So don't dress Claudius in villain's clothes or have him behave furtively. Don't short-circuit the main current.

Some well-meaning teachers do their pupils grave disservice by making them read a play when the students are about to see it in a theater. Do such teachers think plays on stage are better if you already know them? How contrary to a playwright's intentions! Or do such teachers believe students can't comprehend words spoken out loud, and might be confused with all that color and movement? Alas, poor student!

Don't deprive students (or anyone else) of theater's greatest pleasure: the delicious, often suspenseful thirst to know what comes next. Imagine seeing *The Merchant of Venice* not knowing in advance if Shylock will win or lose. And imagine a teacher (or textbook) undoing that pleasure.

In our *not knowing* lies the play's adventure. Don't have Claudius look murd'rous daggers behind Hamlet's back, or let students read *The Merchant of Venice* before they see it, or write program notes telling that Godot never comes. Don't put a synopsis in the audience's hands: "The story thus far. Claudius has murdered Hamlet's father in order to gain the throne of Denmark." If Shakespeare wanted the audience to know it to begin with, he'd have told.

Cherish the audience's ignorance. Don't impose your knowledge of the play's end upon its beginning.

FOCUS: Often the core of dramatic tension resides in keeping information from the audience. Don't negate the tension by premature revelation.

7
Things Theatrical

... amaze indeed
The very faculty of eyes and ears.
Hamlet 2.2.565–66

Things theatrical are all things that elicit strong audience response. A good joke is theatrical. So is a powerfully sad ending, or an evocative costume or language, or a voice that rings. A scene structured so tautly the audience leans forward the whole time is theatrical; so is a yellow mamba coiled beneath the heroine's chair, or a ghost about to say what you have been manipulated into wanting to hear, or a Greek king discovering what he's done to his father and has been doing with his mother.

Something theatrical keeps the audience in the theater: sharp suspense, keen interest, great fun, powerful importance, deep feeling. Something theatrical is good theater. Something that isn't, isn't. Theatrical is the opposite of boring.

Theatricality does not mean cheap effect, though cheap effects (like yellow mambas under chairs) can be theatrical. So can Shakespeare's loftiest moments (and his lowest). Theatricality has nothing to do with good or bad, high or low, art or trash. Crummy strip shows in two-bit joints can be theatrical—as well as the exquisite last scene of *Cyrano de Bergerac*.

Playwrights know that some things may be theatrical and others may not. A lack of action, for instance, usually is not. Sermonizing or lengthy philosophical speeches without situational motivation are rarely theatrical. Men dis-

35

guised as women (or vice-versa) are usually theatrical. Sword fights, lovers seeing each other for the first (or last) time, and death scenes are usually theatrical. Conflict is almost always theatrical, and hardly anything can be theatrical without it.

Novelty is theatrical. Nudity was theatrical for a while, but the novelty wore off.

Change is theatrical. We pay attention to alteration. The change from a small scene of two or three characters to a massive court scene of fifty is in itself theatrical.

For script analysis, identification of theatrical elements is important because good playwrights put their most important material into their most theatrical moments. Shakespeare, as we shall see, goes to intricate lengths to make theatrical the Ghost's speech of act 1, scene 5 because its content is so important. Anything important must be made theatrical so the audience will notice it.

If you are a playwright, don't let your most important material fall between your theatrical moments, like keys through a sewer grating. Theatricality is not trimming. It is the heart, the primary communicator.

Fireworks are theatrical. So is a devastating exit line. The success of a play rests on the impact of its theatricality. If you fail to spot those elements when you read, then you can't get them onto the stage, and neither you nor your audience will quite know what the play is about.

What you don't know won't help you.

FOCUS: *Something is* theatrical *when it garners great audience attention and involvement. Playwrights put their most important material into the play's most theatrical moments, thus taking advantage of heightened audience attention. Identifying the theatrical elements of a play helps discover what the playwright considers important.*

Part Two

Methods

8

Exposition

Your exposition misinterpreting,
We might proceed to cancel of your days.
Pericles 1.1.112–13

An audience knows nothing, to start with. Yet before the action goes far, the audience must be given certain information or nothing can make sense.

That information usually begins with the nature of the play's world in its initial stasis. Where are we? What is it like? What is the situation? What are the time and period? Then we need information about the people and their basic relationships. Who are all these people? What have they to do with each other? And what are they doing here?

The revelation of such necessary information is exposition.

There are two kinds of *exposition*. The first involves information known to everyone on stage, such as: it is Denmark, it is the middle of the night, and the old King Hamlet is recently dead. The playwright's task is to convey that information to the audience.

The second kind of exposition involves information known by only some or one of the characters. The playwright's task in this case is to furnish reason for the knowledgeable character to convey the information to others on stage so the audience can hear. (In classical Greek tragedy the messenger accomplished this). There are more sophisticated techniques, as we shall see.

39

The first kind of exposition—information known to all or most of the characters—is difficult to write well. That is because, as we have seen (in section 5), anything said on stage must stem from something the character wants. But if everyone already knows the information, how could saying it help anyone get what he or she wants? "Hi, John, you who are, as you know, my twin brother," is one awkward result; no actor breathes who can breathe life into such a line. Much of a playwright's ability is revealed by the skill with which this particular difficulty is overcome.

Be on the lookout for sloppy or awkward exposition technique; it is an easy way to spot deficiencies that other elements in the play may suffer from too. "Hello," says the maid picking up the telephone, "this is the large, empty Crumfort mansion on a dark and stormy February night. Oh good evening, Mr. Crumfort, I thought you were enroute to Calcutta." Or, "Sarah! How are you? I haven't seen you since our unfortunate divorce three years ago tonight in Albany." When plays begin like this, be wary of what follows.

There's something worse yet: plays with expositional information that serves no direct purpose. Some writers fill actors' mouths with trivia, hoping the trivia will accumulate into "atmosphere," "local color," or "a sense of time and place." This is a build-up of reality by endless chatty details. Unhappily, irrelevant details build irrelevant reality.

But with a writer you trust, assume the exposition's information is directly relevant to the action.

There is nothing gradual or cumulative about the presentation of exposition relevant to the action, nor do you wait long for it. Read just the first seven lines of *King Lear:*

> *Kent:* I thought the King had more affected the Duke of Albany than Cornwall.
> *Gloucester:* It did always seem so to us, but now in the division of the kingdom it appears not which of the Dukes he values most, for equalities are so weighed that curiosity in neither can make choice of either's moiety.

The play is only fifty-three words old and Shakespeare has already told us a crucial piece of exposition: Lear has already decided how to apportion his kingdom. The planned public contest in which his daughters shall vie with each other to show who loves him most is mere formality, a *ceremony*. It's not a contest to determine which daughter shall get the biggest chunk of kingdom.

Oddly, this information is usually missed. Most productions stage scene one as a contest instead of a public relations stunt. This is not due to different interpretation. It is because of blatant failure to see exposition. Two and two make four. A different answer might be interesting, but it's not arithmetic.

Failure to read carefully results in weak staging. Exhumation of the Bard would reveal him decomposing on his stomach. The first seven lines of *King Lear* are crucial exposition directly related to and explaining the shape of action to come. Those lines are not filler to create local color or background.

Look at how much information we get in *Hamlet*'s first dozen lines (mostly information known by the majority of the characters before us): we learn where we are, and we learn part of the story leading to the present. We learn that a wandering spirit has twice come to these battlements, that it is midnight, that these characters are loyal to the throne of Denmark, and when we actually see the wandering spirit (line 41), we learn that it looks very like "the King that's dead." This is a great deal of information, all of it clearly connected to the action. So far so good. But at line 60 the information *seems* irrelevant, so many readers ignore it:

Such was the very armour he had on
When he the ambitious Norway combated.
So frown'd he once, when in an angry parle
He smote the sledded Polacks on the ice.
'Tis strange.

Indeed 'tis strange! Norway? "Polacks"? A few lines later comes information that seems even less relevant: a history

of Denmark's latest conflict with Norway. This is more detail, thinks the careless reader, than anyone can want—so
the careless reader skims. It is little wonder that the careless reader will never have the vaguest notion what young
Fortinbras has to do with the play. Yet before play's end,
Fortinbras, Hamlet's parallel, will march from Norway
across Denmark to fight "Polacks." So can we assume Fortinbras has a lot to do with this play? Yes, but you'll never
find out what if you skim the exposition that doesn't seem
immediately relevant.

Assume every morsel of exposition is essential to the action of the play—even that which may seem irrelevant. *Try
to discover connections; try hard before giving up, or you
might miss the whole point.*

The second kind of exposition—presentation of information only one character knows—is less difficult for playwrights to do effectively. Most primitively, this kind of exposition is handled by messenger—a neutral character
with no connection to the action except for his message de-
livery: "My Lord, I have come from the castle where the
raging Goths and Visigoths . . ."

A more sophisticated (and more effective) way: the "messenger" is relevant to the action for reasons above and beyond his information. An important character reveals expositional information as a tool to get another character to
do something.

For example, the ghost of Hamlet's father has expositional information. The audience needs the information to
understand the play's action. But this ghost doesn't care
about the audience. His concern is only to use the information about his murder by Claudius to get Hamlet to *do*
something: to seek revenge. The Ghost gives Hamlet information about the past to propel Hamlet into action *now*.
This is the most effective way to present exposition: *use the
past to propel* (not merely explain) *present action*. Be certain
you spot it when the playwright has done it. Read Ibsen, a
master of this technique. It is a technique which does two
things: first, it conveys information the audience needs,
and second, it launches action.

In *Oedipus Tyrannos* this technique is used almost as late as the climax.

This technique is often used for the most important exposition. The Ghost's tale in act 1, scene 5 of *Hamlet* contains far more important information than the number of times the Ghost has been there, or the way it is dressed, or the history of the Poland/Norway/Denmark troubles. Because of its importance, Shakespeare uses a powerful attention-getting device to make us listen to every word. This device, the central building block of theatricality, is described in the next section. For now, understand the need to pay extra attention to exposition when a playwright uses powerful techniques to make us listen. Such techniques have to be used sparingly and selectively; so when one is used (by a writer you trust), assume it is for an especially important reason.

For example, the first seven lines of *King Lear* are extremely important; so Shakespeare took care his audience couldn't miss them. He started the play with them, which gives them a great deal of focus. The focus does not work on twentieth-century audiences, because we do not know the Lear story from other sources. But Shakespeare's audience knew it well. In other versions, familiar to London in 1604, the contest scene is really a contest: whichever daughter says she loves Lear most will win the most land. Shakespeare knew his major change would attract attention, particularly when placed right at the start of the play. It is like opening a stage version of *Cinderella* with information that the stepsisters are very nice, and the stepmother is generous and kind, particularly to Cinderella.

However it is handled, good exposition reveals no more nor no less than everything necessary for the audience to fathom the beginnings of the play's action. The reader who skims exposition, impatient to get on with the play, will have only a vague idea of how or why the action starts and will misunderstand events right to the end.

FOCUS: Exposition is the revelation of information needed by the audience to understand the play's action. There are two *kinds. The first is of information the characters all know. (It's Denmark.) The second is of information not shared by all the characters. At its best, such exposition involves the use of information by one character to propel another into action.*

9

Forwards: Hungry for Next

I will forward with my device.
Love's Labor's Lost 5.2.662

The most obvious is most neglected: audiences can be caught by the scruff of the neck and held wriggling the entire evening. Simply use some device or other to arouse in them the thirst to find out what's *next*.

A forward is anything that arouses an audience's interest in things yet to come. Playwrights want the audience hooked not on the present but the *future*.

Forwards are used in every kind of writing, dramatic and nondramatic—but in drama they are not optional. The reader of a novel may be allowed greater interest in the present than the future, but in a theater different conditions prevail. We must maneuver into unison the attention-rhythms of many different sorts of people, despite individual variations in things like concentration span, interest, taste, understanding, emotional and intellectual involvement, physical comfort, attitudes, and mood. The playwright must seize *control* of audience attention.

Book readers can control their own rhythms. They can read for half an hour, get up, pace, eat a banana, count stamps, reread a chapter, skim (or skip) a paragraph or page or chapter of lesser interest, discuss the thing with someone, throw the book out the window at a bird or into the fireplace, or put it down for a week.

But in a theater, if the audience tires of watching twenty minutes before intermission, the show is in trouble. Thus, skilled playwrights load scenes with forwards, so no matter how strong the scene (or weak) the audience is maneuvered into an eagerness to remain to see what's next.

If you are home reading a book and have to go to the bathroom, you stop reading and go, or you take the book with you. Yet, remarkably, few theater practitioners or theorists note that at any given time a good portion of any audience has to go to the bathroom. This characteristic of live theater has obtained since its origins (unless classic Athenians knew something we don't). So if a show fails to sufficiently tantalize the audience with what is coming next, many will wander out and spend act 1, scene 5 in the bathroom, or at best will think more about personal biological needs than the play.

An audience cannot pace, take a break, eat a banana or . . . anything. *The poor audience must sit still.* The playwright, unlike poet or novelist, must make the audience *want* to sit still. Without forwards the audience will be ready to rise at the end of the next speech. This is a major difference between dramatic and other forms of literature. When we are dying to know what is coming next, we sit still and pay attention. When we aren't, we don't—we would rather do almost anything than sit still. If you do not believe it, sit for three hours while someone reads *Paradise Lost* aloud to you. You will fidget. You won't last, because there are few forwards.

Some forms of nondramatic literature are intended for reading aloud: Chaucer, Homer, *Beowulf.* All are full of forwards. Hemingway is not, nor Dickens, Faulkner, Pope. But Shakespeare is, and Sophocles. Both use forwards on every page—as do not only the giants but almost every playwright, modern or not, you can name. (A playwright who writes without forwards will probably never be a playwright anyone can name.)

A forward is any of a myriad of devices, techniques, tricks, maneuvers, manipulations, appetizers, tantalizers, teasers, that make an audience eager for what's coming up. If you miss a script's forwards you miss the playwright's most distinctive, gripping tool. What stripper does not know that the *promise* of nudity more excites an audience than does nudity itself?

Half the pleasure is in the anticipation.

Not only do forwards keep us interested, but *forwards also focus attention where the playwright wants it.* Our attention is made keenest (by a skilled writer) where it needs to be keenest. This provides a reliable analytic method to discover what the playwright thinks important. If Shakespeare creates an elaborate set of forwards to specially focus attention on something, that something must be crucial.

Let us examine a set of forwards Shakespeare uses to (1) arouse our interest in what's next and (2) heighten and focus that interest to make us pay optimum attention right where he wants it.

Hamlet: not until line 685 of the play does the Ghost speak. That's about half the length of a Greek tragedy. A less-skilled playwright would have had the Ghost's speech at line 1. But Shakespeare delays so he can create a set of clear, simple forwards. They rivet attention not merely on the Ghost's presence, but on what the Ghost has to say.

More has been written about *Hamlet* than about any other piece of English literature. Somewhere in all that scrutiny the obvious has been lost, so you must find it for yourself. Begin, for example, by looking for elements that arouse interest in the Ghost before its first entrance. The first line of the play—numbered *1* in most editions—is, "Who's there?" Immediately we want to know who—or what—may be wandering these parapets. And just a few lines later Horatio has a line calculated by Shakespeare to whet our curiosity:

What, has this thing appeared again tonight?

Horatio could have said "ghost" but "this thing" is less definite so more tantalizing. For six or seven more lines we are enticed, eager now for every new bit of information about "this thing."

> *Horatio:*   What, has this thing appeared again tonight?
> *Bernardo:* I have seen nothing.
>
> [21-22]

But that won't relax the audience for a moment, because
the audience knows Bernardo can have seen nothing—he
has only just arrived. The implication that excites
anticipation—and thus attention—is that "this thing"
could show up any minute.

> *Marcellus:* Horatio says 'tis but our fantasy,
>   And will not let belief take hold of him
>   Touching this dreaded sight twice seen of us;
>
> [23-25]

("This thing" is now a shade more definite: a "dreaded
sight." Whetter and whetter are our appetites.)

>   Therefore I have entreated him along
>   With us to watch the minutes of this night,
>   That if again this apparition come
>   He may approve our eyes and speak to it.
> *Horatio:* Tush, tush, 'twill not appear.
>
> [26-30]

The audience knows a few things Horatio doesn't, so has
less reason to doubt. First, the audience knows this is a
play, and that when a play whets an appetite for something
it usually pays off. Second, the audience knows it is
midnight—a detail revealed in line 6 of the play. Horatio
may not believe in apparitions, nor perhaps does everyone
in the audience, but the audience knows that if an apparition is to be (so to speak), it is most likely to be at midnight.

Better yet, Shakespeare has now set up forwards that
promise us a delicious moment when Horatio, the rational
unbeliever ("Tush, tush, 'twill not appear"), confronts the
thing he does not believe in. So before the Ghost's first appearance, the audience is made eager for two highly theatrical events: the appearance of a dreadful apparition, and
its confrontation with a man who avows it won't appear.

If the first forty lines are staged as introductory chatter the audience will not be hooked, their appetites not whetted. So the Ghost's appearance will have small effect despite all the fog, creepy sound cues, and eerie lights the production can muster. But if the forwards of the first forty lines are staged clearly, the audience will be leaning forward full of anticipation and careful attention. The Ghost, sans fog, sans lights, sans effects will be most theatrically effective. Lights, fog, and sound may be used, of course, but don't neglect the core of what Shakespeare wrote: simple, skilled, effective *forwards*.

Yet that's but the start. Shakespeare's real task is to make us listen with excruciating care to what the Ghost says in its speech to Hamlet (in act 1, scene 5). But we have entered the theater not caring one way or the other about this Ghost, so Shakespeare takes six hundred lines to maneuver us into caring, to make certain that the theatricality of the Ghost's mere presence doesn't overweigh its crucial words. See how obvious and repeating is Shakespeare's maneuver:

> *Horatio*   [to the Ghost]: What art thou that usurpst this
> time of night,
> Together with that fair and warlike form
> In which the majesty of buried Denmark
> Did sometimes march? *By heaven I charge thee
> speak!*
> *Marcellus:* It is offended.
> *Bernardo:*   See, it stalks away.
> *Horatio:*   Stay! *Speak, speak,* I charge thee *speak!*
> *Marcellus:* 'Tis gone and *will not answer.*
>
> [46–52;emphasis added]

Five times in four lines we are made to understand that the Ghost *refuses to speak.* What better way for Shakespeare to maneuver us (and for the Ghost to maneuver Horatio) into wanting to know what the Ghost has to say?

Seventy-four lines later the Ghost returns. In the meantime we've received a great deal of exposition: the material about Denmark and Norway, about the Ghost's identity in real life, about the current dire political situation, and

about the appearance of dreadful apparitions portending
foul events (lines 112–26 tell of the walking dead squeaking
and gibbering in the Roman streets just before Caesar's as-
sassination). Eager curiosity about the Ghost makes us listen carefully to all that concentrated exposition—
information in which we would have had little interest and
to which we would have paid little attention had Shakespeare not maneuvered us into *wanting to know*. The maneuvers make *us* want to do the work.

So by the Ghost's second entrance we know much.

Horatio tries again, and as he does our desire to hear
what the Ghost might have to say is increased.

The forward is now repeated like a tolling bell, in a
rhythmic repetition that an audience can't miss:

> *Horatio* [to the Ghost]: Stay, illusion!
>   If thou hast any sound or use of voice,
>   *Speak to me.*
>   If there be any good thing to be done
>   That may to thee do ease, and grace to me
>   *Speak to me.*
>   If thou art privy to thy country's fate
>   Which happily foreknowing may avoid,
>   *O speak!*
>   Or if thou hast uphoarded in thy life
>   Extorted treasure in the womb of earth
>   For which, they say, you spirits oft walk in death,
>   *Speak* of it, stay and *speak*.
>   [127–39; emphasis added]

Five more "speaks" do their work on us. We are primed
for the Ghost to speak. Instead, we hear the cock crow and
the Ghost stalks off.

We are whetted but unfed. Yet Shakespeare isn't through
with us. By the time he lets the Ghost speak, we will be the
keenest listeners an audience can be. The forwards continue as Horatio tells Hamlet what has passed:

> *Hamlet:* Did you not *speak* to it?
> *Horatio:*   My Lord, I did,
>   *But answer made it none.* Yet once methought
>   It lifted up its head and did address

Itself to motion *like as it would speak,*
But even then the morning cock crew loud,
And at the sound it shrunk in haste away
And vanished from our sight.

[1.2.214–20; emphasis added]

How excruciating that we *almost* heard it speak!
As scene 2 ends we get another tantalizing hint of what's
to come. Hamlet does not think the Ghost forebodes some
ill of the future, but rather something already done, now
hidden:

Hamlet: Would the night were come.
Till then sit still, my soul. *Foul deeds will rise*
Though all the earth o'erwhelm them to men's eyes.

[emphasis added]

Those last two lines rhyme. Most commonly, it is considered that such rhyming couplets round off and cap the
scenes they end. But in fact they do quite the opposite: *they
tell us not what's passed but hint at what's coming.* They
rhyme in order to be conspicuous in an otherwise un-
rhymed scene; being conspicuous they can be forwards—
tantalizing us, whetting our appetites for what is to come.
"Foul deeds will rise/Though all the earth o'erwhelm them
to men's eyes"—so the end of scene 2 itches us with even
more curiosity to hear what the Ghost will say, what it will
reveal. Now we think the Ghost will unearth some horrible
deed. We are ready to hang on each of the Ghost's words.
But Shakespeare's not done yet! Look at act 1, scene 4 and
the start of act 1, scene 5. Put yourself in the audience's
frame of mind: you are desperate to hear what the Ghost
has to say.

Enter Ghost

Horatio: Look, my Lord, it comes!
Hamlet: Angels and ministers of grace defend us!
Be thou a spirit of health, or goblin damned,
Bring with thee airs from heaven or blasts from
hell,
Be thy intents wicked or charitable,

> Thou comest in such a questionable shape
> That I will speak to thee. I'll call thee Hamlet,
> King, father, royal Dane! O, answer me.
>
> [1.4.38–45]

Look at that last sentence as it should appear in the stage manager's prompt book:

Hamlet: I'll call thee Hamlet.
    [no response]
    King!
    [no response]
    Father!
    [no response]
    Royal Dane!
    [no response]
    O, *answer* me!

How many Hamlets have rushed through those appellations never waiting for response, then senselessly have cried "O answer me!" as if they had given the damnèd thing a chance to? But the Hamlet Shakespeare wrote wants answer, is violently in search of answer. The whetted audience, because Shakespeare used forwards, wants answer just as much. So Hamlet continues:

Hamlet: Let me not burst in ignorance, but *tell*
    Why thy canonized bones, hearsed in death,
    Have burst their cerements; *why* the sepulchre
    Wherein we saw thee quietly interred
    Hath op'd his ponderous and marble jaws
    To cast thee up again. *What may this mean,*
    That thou, dead corse, again in complete steel
    Revisits thus the glimpses of the moon,
    Making night hideous, and we fools of nature
    So horridly to shake our disposition
    With thoughts beyond the reaches of our souls?
    Say why is this?
    [no response]
            Wherefore?
    [no response]
               What should we do?
    [the Ghost] beckons [Hamlet to follow]
               [46–57; emphasis added]

For the next thirty-five lines Hamlet fights to hear what the Ghost has to say. The other characters try to dissuade Hamlet. Shakespeare has maneuvered us into wanting exactly what his main character wants. Our fate, for the moment, is Hamlet's. For us to get what we want (to hear the Ghost's words), Hamlet must follow the Ghost despite the obstacles:

> *Horatio:* It beckons you to go away with it
>   As if it some impartment did desire
>   To you alone.
>   [58-60]

(I.e., as if it wanted *to tell you* something in private—this is yet another forward.)

> *Marcellus:* Look with what courteous action
>   It waves you to a more removed ground,
>   But do not go with it.
> *Horatio:* No, by no means.
> *Hamlet:* It will not speak, then I will follow it.

("Good!" thinks the audience, wanting to hear what the Ghost will say.)

> *Horatio:* Do not, my Lord.

("Bad!" thinks the audience.)

> *Hamlet:* Why, what should be the fear?
>   I do not set my life at a pin's fee.
>   And for my soul, what can it do to that,
>   Being a thing immortal as itself?
>   It waves me forth again; I'll follow it.

(Listen to the obstacles Horatio tries to throw in Hamlet's way:)

> *Horatio:* What if it tempt you toward the flood, my Lord,
>   Or to the dreadful summit of the cliff
>   That beetles o'er his base into the sea,
>   And there assume some other horrible form
>   Which might deprive your sovereignty of
>   reason
>   And draw you into madness?

(Madness? "Hmm," thinks the audience, "what have we here? What might this lead to? What's *next*?")

Horatio [continuing]:   Think of it.
   The very place puts toys of desperation,
   Without more motive, into every brain
   That looks so many fathoms to the sea
   And hears it roar beneath.
Hamlet: It waves me still.—
   Go on! I'll follow thee!
Marcellus: You shall not go, my Lord.
Hamlet: Hold off your hands.
Horatio: Be ruled, you shall not go.
Hamlet: My fate cries out
   And makes each petty artery in this body
   As hardy as the Nemean lion's nerve.
   Still I am called. Unhand me, gentlemen.
   By heaven, I'll make a ghost of him that lets
    [prevents] me.
   I say away!—[*to Ghost*] Go on. I'll follow thee.
             [60–86]

Finally Hamlet is off after the Ghost. Now we are about to get what we've been thirsty for:

Hamlet [to Ghost]: Wither will thou lead me?
   Speak. I'll go no further.
Ghost: Mark me.
             [1.5.1–2]

("Mark me" may be one of dramatic literature's greatest understatements.)

Shakespeare is not subtle. He explodes a set of forwards by having the Ghost exhorted over and over and over to speak. Has anything in the play been repeated as much?

Shakespeare has gone to those lengths because the Ghost's speech contains the play's major exposition; the action of the play depends upon the audience apprehending every detail. Because Shakespeare has made the audience so hungry to hear, it eagerly does the work necessary to listen carefully.

For an example of how a relative detail is important: the Ghost directs Hamlet not to exact revenge from his mother. If we miss that detail, then Hamlet's behavior toward Gertrude as the play progresses will seem confusing and irrational. If you understand the device of forwarding, then you can stage the play so the audience won't miss a word of the Ghost's speech. On the other hand you can ignore Shakespeare's six-hundred-line technical effort and present a Ghost totally reliant on stage effects for attention. In that case you might as well eliminate the Ghost's words and have it wave its arms, shriek, gibber, and go boo.

Strong exploitation of the forwards provided will enable a production to catapult itself and its audience into the torrent of action that is *Hamlet.* At the same time, maneuvering the audience into paying close attention to the Ghost's speech establishes a structural and emotional base that can last the entire performance.

Forwarding Couplets

Let us look at other forwards. One kind has already been touched on: rhymed couplets that end many Shakespeare scenes: "Till then sit still, my soul. Foul deeds will rise/ Though all the earth o'erwhelm them to men's eyes" (*Hamlet* 1.2.256–57). Let us look at a few to see how they propel audience attention *forward.*

From *Hamlet,* act 2, scene 2:

Hamlet: I'll have grounds
            More relative than this. The play's the thing
            Wherein *I'll catch the conscience of the King.*

                        [emphasis added]

And we await the event eagerly.

From *Hamlet,* act 4, scene 4:

Hamlet: O, from this time forth
            My thoughts be bloody, or be nothing worth.

That couplet doesn't rhyme, but it did in 1601. It ends a
scene wherein Hamlet has seen Fortinbras' troops from
Norway. The troops have had some effect on Hamlet. But
Hamlet is now forced off to England—seemingly leaving
the action. So lest our attention flag, Shakespeare gives us
something to look forward to: bloody thoughts mean un-
abated action.

> From *Othello*, act 1, scene 3:
>
> *Iago:* I have't. It is engend'red. *Hell and night*
> *Must bring this monstrous birth to the world's light.*
>
> [emphasis added]

Even if you've never read the play your curiosity is aroused
about what's coming up. A few scenes later (act 5, scene 1)
Iago says of the night to come:

> *Iago:* This is the night
> That either makes me, or foredoes me quite.

Shakespeare dangles carrots in front of us continually.
You can find few if any moments in his works when one
forward or another is not in effect.

The use of the forwarding rhymed couplet to end a scene
is a practice peculiar to Elizabethan playwrights and a few
imitators, so in itself it isn't that important. But the forwarding principle *is*, so examine many couplets to become
expert in understanding and making use of forwards. And
you will gain an added familiarity with the plays.

Other Forwards

Plays contain tiny forwards to keep us in anticipation
from moment to moment, and major forwards that deal
with the play's overall action. Sooner or later, the play implicitly promises, the major opposing forces will meet head
on. Sooner or later Hamlet will confront Claudius. Anticipation of this confrontation can hold the audience all the
way through the evening. A production that takes no pains

to make the audience eager for the confrontation will be boring no matter how fascinating its constituent parts.

Shakespeare goes so far as to tease us by *almost* presenting a Hamlet/Claudius confrontation (as he teased us by having the Ghost *almost* speak just as the cock crew)—but Hamlet tiptoes away to leave the king praying (3.3). Over and over Shakespeare whets us for the ultimate confrontation at play's end.

For any play, promise of the ultimate confrontation must be used to arouse audience eagerness. Sooner or later Macbeth has to pay the piper, and we must be made to want to see it.

The audience knows that Edmund and Edgar, the odd-coupled brothers in *King Lear*, eventually must have it out. So must Lear and Cordelia. The audience must be maneuvered, wooed, cajoled into wanting to be witness. *Herein lies the tension of a production.* It is precisely tension's lack that ruins more productions than any other single problem.

Sometimes the promise of a forward is not fulfilled. What we've been made eager for never comes to pass. But that is okay. The playwright is not cheating. Early in Chekhov's *The Cherry Orchard* someone fiddles with a gun. In those days the presence of a gun early in a play assured a shooting by play's end, so the audience waited and waited for it. But no one in *The Cherry Orchard* gets shot. We've been filled with anticipation for something that never happens. (This is what many people mean by "Chekhovian.") But in spite of the fact no shooting takes place, *the effect of the forward is the same:* the audience has been maneuvered into paying close attention.

Sooner or later, hope Vladimir and Estragon, Godot will arrive. We're made as eager for the arrival as they are, but the promise is never fulfilled. No matter; the anticipation served its purpose in carrying us through the play. (Of course, *Waiting for Godot* is now a classic, so we sophisticates sit in the audience in our superior knowledge that Godot will never come. So we are more likely to be bored than the lucky audiences that saw the play in its early years, filled with the delicious, overwhelming tension that at any moment Godot might show up.)

In *Oedipus Tyrannos* the audience walks into the theater already knowing the protagonist's awful truth. Even the Athenians on Sophocles' opening night knew. Unlike *The Cherry Orchard*'s nonshooting, unlike the nonarrival of Godot, the ultimate expectation in *Oedipus Tyrannos* will occur—and we know it for certain. But the expectation is not merely the surfacing of a truth we already know and fully comprehend. What we are made eager to see is how Oedipus will react when *he* finds out his awful truth. When this proud, secure, moral, happy, fortunate family man and hero discovers the horror lurking beneath his sheets and back at the crossroads, *what will he do?* If you cannot help make us eager to find that out, you have no business working on the play. And you will give us an irrelevant blinding.

A few years ago on television's *All in the Family,* everyone's favorite bigot, Archie Bunker, opened his front door to greet, for the first time, his new neighbor. The scene ended with Archie's discovery that he and his neighbor were not of the same race. It is doubtful a dial in America was touched during the commercial. All wanted to see what bigot Archie would do *next.*

Whether by Shakespeare, Sophocles, the writers of *All in the Family*, Beckett, or Chekhov—any script that holds an audience is filled with forwards.

Some are trivial. A psychiatrist in *Equus* tosses off a line. On his way to visit for the first time the home of the boy he's trying to treat, he remarks, "If there's any tension over religion [in that home] it should be evident on a sabbath evening!"

A throwaway line, seemingly, but it makes us pay closer attention to the scene in the boy's home, hoping there will be some tension about religion. We are promised, in return for close attention, a theatrical scene—and that is what we get. As a bonus, our attention is directed to an important topic of the scene.

Equus is a fine work to study for its forwards. It is crammed with them. From the first image our curiosity is aroused; so we pay close, eager attention to things that probably held little interest for us when we entered the theater. Find and examine the many forwards in *Equus*. Peter Shaffer is a master of them. You'll learn a lot.

Forwards make us sit still and be eager, and they focus us on what the playwright considers the most important elements. If I tell you that the next chapter has the funniest joke in the English language, a piece of outrageous pornography that can arouse anyone, the scariest vampire tale ever told, the secret of how to get a job in the theater, *and* a photo of me writing this book, you will probably read the next chapter—whether I am lying or not.

That's a *forward*.

FOCUS: Dramatic tension requires that the audience desire to find out what is coming up. The greater the desire, the greater—and more active—the audience's involvement. Playwrights employ many techniques—forwards—to increase the thirst for what's coming up. Such techniques are also a key to spotting elements the playwright considers important.

10
Missing Persons (Character)

Who's there?

Hamlet 1.1.1

Character analysis and development are highly specialized in drama. Few methods useful to nondramatic writing help, and some hinder by yielding invalid results.

This is because character in drama is revealed in one way: action, that which a person does—*deeds*. The very word *deed* means *truth*, in*deed* it does. Human beings have always assumed personality is revealed through deeds. Other forms of character revelation are so rare in drama that they employ special conventions. (There is an exception, but a dangerous one, as we shall see.)

Character consists of all the qualities, traits, and features that create the nature of a person and distinguish that person from another person.

Character answers "Who am I?" The minimum answer is name. "Who are you?" asks the dentist's appointment secretary. The patient gives a name—for the circumstances, a sufficient answer. The maximum answer is endless. The patient could elaborate forever, telling who he is for hours, days, months.

Somewhere between the minimum (name only) and the maximum (unlimited self-chatter) falls the amount of information necessary to create character in literature. Nondramatic literature usually offers much more character information than does drama. In fact, drama offers hardly any. You probably know more about most acquaintances than *anyone* knows about Hamlet. This difference between how much is known about acquaintances and how little is known about Hamlet is owing to something obvious about drama—obvious and usually ignored:

There is no such person as Hamlet.

There is no such person as King Lear, or Willy Loman, or Oedipus, or Archie Bunker. They do not exist. They never did. They are minimally extant in scripts, skeletal accumulations of carefully selected traits. A scripted character is comprised of remarkably little—because *the nature of any stage character is heavily determined by the actor in the part.* Olivier is Olivier, Brando is Brando. One actor's Hamlet can be but little like the other's even if both actors use identical interpretations—because Olivier is little like Brando.

Play characters are not *real.* You cannot discover everything about them from the script. The playwright cannot give much, because the more that is given, the harder it is to cast the part. The playwright must leave most of the character *blank* to accommodate the nature of the actor. This is one reason novels are longer than plays: novels need no gaps for actors. So there is more of Ahab than of Oedipus; in fact, there is more Miss Marple than Oedipus. *Scripts contain bones, not people.*

Good playwrights limit their choice of bones to those which make the character unique. Onto that uniqueness the actor hangs the rest of the human being.

The bones—the carefully selected character traits included in the script—are revealed via action. Devices such as a chorus, or narrator, or presentation of interior thoughts via soliloquy, or exposition (often awkwardly shoved into mouths: "I am your honest but inept twin brother, as you know") are peripheral, call for special conventions, and rarely offer information not revealed elsewhere—and better—through action. Such devices should not be ignored, but they are auxiliary to action as a source of information.

Remember that action doesn't mean gesture or jumping

up and down. Action results from what a character *does* to get what he or she wants (motivation) in spite of obstacles. The first step in delving into character is to find out (1) what the character wants, (2) what is in the character's way (obstacle), and (3) what the character does or is willing to do to satisfy the want. (This step, of course, comes after the obvious: name, age, sex, station and situation. For example, Hamlet is in his early thirties—as is revealed by careful reading of act 5, scene 1—is male, is Prince of Denmark, and is mourning his father. Don't ignore the obvious. Many miss that Hamlet's a prince, despite the play's title—*Hamlet, Prince of Denmark*—so they don't note that a prince might have certain expectations and certain things expected of him. This has a lot to do with the play.)

Once the obvious is noted, study what the character does.

A character's self-description, or how others in a play describe a character, is not reliable for the simple real-life reason that what people *say* is not reliable. Polonius *says* things about Hamlet:

> *Polonius* [to Claudius and Gertrude]:
> I will be brief. Your noble son is mad.
> Mad, call I it, for to define true madness
> What is't but to be nothing else but mad? . . .
> That he's mad, 'tis true.
>
> [2.2.92–97]

After all, reasons Polonius, didn't Hamlet, socks downgyved, talk weirdly to Ophelia? And because Polonius (of all people) labels Hamlet insane, generations of readers and critics agree. It is easy to agree when merely reading, because readers easily make the error of focusing more on what is said than what is done. But an audience focuses on what is done, and plays are written for audiences.

What is done? For one thing, Hamlet, socks downgyved, talks weirdly to Ophelia *in order to maneuver Polonius into thinking he's insane.* The maneuver is so successful that not only Polonius but generations of reading commentators are convinced. These commentators are as misled as Rosencrantz and Guildenstern are when Hamlet claims he's melancholy:

Hamlet [to Rosencrantz and Guildenstern]:
> I have of late—but wherefore I know not—lost all
> my mirth, forgone all custom of exercises, and in-
> deed it goes so heavily with my disposition that
> this goodly frame, the earth, seems to me a sterile
> promontory.
>
> [2.2.295–99]

Many besides Rosencrantz and Guildenstern take Hamlet here at his word. But has not Hamlet in the previous
instant discovered that Rosencrantz and Guildenstern have
been sent to spy on him? Hamlet has every reason to lie to
them, *and he does.*

Self-description cannot be trusted because characters
often have reason to mislead others. Nor can a character's
description of another character be trusted because the de-
scriber could be mistaken or lying.

Description must be validated by examination of action.
Action either verifies description, rendering description re-
dundant, or it reveals that the description is wrong. Re-
dundant or wrong: that is all description can be.

Action/What and Action/Why

What a character does is half the revelation. *Why* the
character does it is the other half.

Hamlet stabs to death a defenseless old man (action/
what). The act seems to reveal that Hamlet is brutal and
unfair. But *why* did he do it? Why kill Polonius? Did he
think it was Claudius behind the arras? If that were the
case, would Hamlet still be revealed as brutal and unfair?
Or if Hamlet knew it was Polonius, might our conclusion
about Hamlet's character be altered by the possibility that
he knew Polonius could have been privy to Claudius'
crime?

I do not kick dogs. I like dogs. It is "out of character" for
me to kick one. But I kick one. Does this mean I don't like
dogs? Not necessarily. Action/what: kicking a dog. Action/
why: the dog is rabid and biting your neck. At risk to myself I try rescuing you.

Or: I like dogs, but not *cute* dogs. I kick cute dogs.

Action/why modifications create different character conclusions.

Avowed Action/Why Versus True Action/Why

The difference between *avowed* action/why and *true* ac-
tion/why often reveals a lot about character. Claudius, having arranged for Hamlet to be murdered in England, tells
Hamlet "why" Hamlet is being sent: he is, claims Claudius,
in danger because he killed Polonius.

> *Claudius:* Hamlet, this deed, for thine especial safety—
> Which we do tender, as we dearly grieve
> For that which thou hast done—must send thee
>   hence
> With fiery quickness. Therefore prepare thyself.
> The bark is ready, and the wind at help,
> Th' associates tend, and every thing is bent
> For England.
> *Hamlet:*   For England.
> *Claudius:*   Ay, Hamlet.
> *Hamlet:*   Good.
> *Claudius:* So is it, if thou knew'st our purposes.
> *Hamlet:* I see a cherub that sees them.
>
> [4.3.40–48]

Hamlet knows the true action/why—or at least he sus-
pects Claudius is up to no good. We see right through a
person when we discover a difference between avowed and
true action/why—both on stage and in life.

To summarize: the beginning and end of character reside
in action—things *shown*, not described by words. Character
is revealed by examining simultaneously action/what and
action/why, and is further revealed in the difference between avowed action/why and true action/why.

In other words: action speaks louder than words, and
talk is cheap.

This does not mean words are unimportant. But they are
suspect when they merely describe. If you say to me,
"Merry Christmas," and I say, "I am a grumpy old fellow
who hates the Yuletide," the theatrical effect is minimal. I

have *described* myself, and audiences tend to pay description little attention. But if you say, "Merry Christmas," and I hurl at you, "Bah! Humbug!" you (and the audience) have seen me in action.

Subjectivity, Character Change, Mystery

Actions on stage that most richly reveal character work in the same way as actions do in real life. You must find them out for yourself because how I interpret what I see differs from how you interpret what you see. Much of what I perceive when I regard you is based on who I am, not just who you are. Objective analysis of character is not possible. *Characterization is partly in the eye of the beholder, because we always judge others in terms of our individual selves.*

Thus, character offers great interpretive latitude. We can agree with each other on plot because it's all in the script and usually unambiguous. We can more or less agree on a play's themes. But rarely can two readers see precisely the same character, because we must judge mere skeleton and because individual judgement is involved.

Nevertheless, the success of theater depends on perception of character. So beware of shortcuts and traps. A particularly insidious trap is the old assertion that character changes during a play. But people in plays don't change any more than people in real life do. If they do we don't believe them. An attitude may change, or a method a character uses; a particular character trait may *seem* to alter, but more likely it is the *situation* that has changed. A better or more efficient or easier or more acceptable way arises of satisfying the same character trait.

For example, Edmund, Edgar's evil brother in *King Lear*, abruptly "repents" at play's end.

> *Edmund:* I pant for life. Some good I mean to do
> Despite of mine own nature.
>
> [5.3.244–45]

Has Edmund, he who has destroyed his father, changed? Has this villain suddenly, because he knows he's dying (or that it's act 5), changed his stripe? Is he really violating his "own nature?"

What has actually happened is more plausible. From the beginning Edmund has wanted to be the equal of his legitimate brother, Edgar. So Edmund embarks on a plot to gain that which keeps him from being equal: Edgar's land. But by act 5 Edgar is revered for his virtue, not his land. Now Edmund must *appear* virtuous to get what he wanted all along: equality to Edgar. It is the same trait, the same desire. Edmund's character has not changed, but a changed situation calls for different tactics. Edmund remains Edmund.

So full circle: to find out character, examine motivation, obstacle, and what the person does or will do to get around the obstacle. Obstacle may change, but overall motivation rarely does. We want what we want, and change only how we try to get it.

Finally: even the best characterizations remain, at core, mysteries. Only lesser dramatists (or lesser psychologists) try to understand or even to perceive the totality of a human being. *A character laid out clearly, rationally, and fully explained is not only impossible, but dull and implausible.* There's nothing like it in real life. Hamlet, Lear, Oedipus remain, ultimately, mysteries—*just as we do in real life to each other and to ourselves.* That mystery may be all we have in common with Medea or Faustus, Macbeth or Cyrano, but it is enough. It is what we all share, our strength and fragility in one. Trying to reduce the ultimate mystery of character to simple, pat mechanics reduces people to incomplete formulae. It does not raise them to life. And the intent of the stage is to raise characters to life.

"Who am I?" No one can answer thoroughly. Yet to help present a character on stage—whether you write, design, direct or act—seize on every concrete morsel of character you can find. And remember that even after decades of intense psychological study and research, no one knows a better way to present or interpret character than through what a person *does*.

Study people in a play as if their lives depended on it. Then add actors. The sum is character.

FOCUS: *Character is revealed primarily by what a character does. Yet even the best of plays presents only a skeleton, because much of what the audience perceives as character has to do with the actor. Moreover, character is drama's most subjective element, because we each perceive a particular character differently, depending on our own natures. The best reading approach is to discover the skeleton of character as revealed by action.*

11

Image

Make my image but an alehouse sign.
Henry VI, Part 2 3.2.81

There are two kinds of communication. The first, generally
the domain of science or philosophy, describes phenomena
one part at a time, element by isolated element, and as
particularly as possible: "Her facial muscles tensed so as to
retract her lips from her teeth, the whiteness of which was
in high contrast to her skin coloring." Dictionary
definitions—for example, this one from the *American Heritage Dictionary*—are usually this first kind of communication:

> Moon: The natural satellite of the earth, visible by reflection
> of sunlight, having a slightly elliptical orbit, approximately 221,600 miles distant at perigee and 252,950 miles
> at apogee. Its mean diameter is 2,160 miles, its mass approximately one-eightieth that of the earth, and its average period of revolution around the earth 29 days 12
> hours 44 minutes calculated with respect to the sun.

The second kind of communication does not deal with a
single element at a time, but rather expresses a collection,
a combination of multiple, simultaneous elements that together express fullness and totality. This is a less precise
but more evocative communication than the first kind. It
belongs to the domain of art. "Her smile was sunrise breaking through a spring blizzard." Or, from *A Midsummer
Night's Dream:*

Theseus: O, methinks, how slow
　　　　This old moon wanes. She lingers my desires
　　　　Like to a step-dame or a dowager.

[1.1.3–5]

The first kind is not better or worse than the second.
They are for different ends. The first *specifies and limits.*
The second *expands, evokes.*
The first kind of communication is concerned with the
thing described. The moon itself is the subject of the dictionary definition. But the second kind—the kind employ-
ing the *image*—is concerned with our *reaction* to the thing
described. The moon shining through forest trees at 4:00
A.M. on a January night can be scientifically described, but
no dictionary can define our reactions to it. Scientific description can express each separate element of fingernails
scraping a blackboard, but the totality of the event (which
must include our reaction) cannot exist in a dictionary. Totality requires multiple, evocative parts—and that is the
function of the image.

"She walked like a sparrow beside her elephant of a husband." Without images, I would need pages to communi-
cate everything that sentence contains. **An image is something we already know or can easily be told that is used to
describe, illuminate, or expand upon something we don't
know or cannot easily be told.** Without images I would
need paragraphs of description, examples, and analysis to
describe how my neighbor drives her car. Yet a single image, *by evoking your reactions to something you already
know,* communicates it in five words: "She doesn't drive,
she aims."

"She left her husband like a bat out of hell." You interpret that image (bat out of hell) a little differently than I
do. This is why everyone's reaction to a work of art is
unique. We are discussing the *un*scientific method, though
we are discussing it more or less scientifically. In scientific
communication ambiguity is bad. Precise definition is
good. *Precision at the expense of totality is for science; total-*

ity at the expense of precision is for art. "She cooks like a chemist"—not much precise information there, but oh how much it says! You can see her at it: how she does it, what her kitchen looks like, even what she might wear. You can guess at her personality, and even speculate about the meals she serves. All that and more is communicated in five words—and communicated slightly differently to every listener.

Images compress: they provide a lot of information in a small space. And the information is limited only by the perception and imagination of the listener. In act 1, scene 1 of *Hamlet*, Bernardo speaks of Horatio's refusal to believe in the apparition:

> *Bernardo:* Let us once again assail your ears
> That are so fortified against our story.
>
> [31–32]

Discover how much is communicated in those few words: nearly a Cecil B. DeMille spectacular describing Horatio's whole attitude and how Bernardo will deal with it. And not accidentally the image is drawn from the situation surrounding the speaker: Denmark is preparing for war, and the scene occurs on an armed battlement.

The effect relies on individual, personal reactions to the battle terms "assail" and "fortified against." The terms evoke slightly different reactions from everyone, depending on his or her associations with them.

Originally image meant something strictly visual: a mirror image, or cave-wall images, or a photographic image—one or another kind of optical reproduction. But now the term means a reproduction in any form of anything we can perceive with our senses, visual or otherwise.

In plays, the reproduction is most often in the form of words, especially when you are reading. You must be able to find and extract the images. "He entered the room like a wave of nausea" is an image: a reproduction of something we can perceive with our senses (nausea). It uses what we know about nausea to evoke something we don't know about: how he entered the room.

Hamlet: How weary, stale, flat and unprofitable
　　　Seem to me all the uses of this world.
　　　Fie on't, ah fie! 'Tis an unweeded garden
　　　That grows to seed. Things rank and gross in nature
　　　Possess it merely.

　　　　　　　　　　　　　　　　[1.2.133–34]

　　The image reproduced: a neglected garden, which most
of us can picture and understand (though each in our personal ways), so we can react to it. Our reactions tell us,
both intellectually and emotionally, of Hamlet's attitude
towards the world. "Unweeded garden," "grows to seed,"
"things rank and gross"—our emotional associations and
responses are as important as the precise intellectual information conveyed. (And if I have grown up in the country, where gardens abound, my associations will be vastly
different from yours if you have grown up in the city with
nothing more than a window box or two.)
　　As a play progresses, emotional responses and associations accumulate. Eventually the accumulation of reactions
helps the audience to emotionally *experience*, not merely
understand. *The simultaneous communication of both understanding and emotional experience is the domain of art.*
　　Understanding alone, without emotional content, without personal reaction being evoked, is the domain of philosophy and science.
　　Understanding and emotional experience can be communicated simultaneously via images—either trivial images that bolster a phrase, or major controlling images to
which you must pay special attention (a collection of glass
animals in a Tennessee Williams play). Find ways to com-
municate these images to your audience, or you will flatten
your production to mere information.

Images in Titles

Remember: your task as reader is to discover the familiar
characteristics of an image that describe and illuminate
the subject. One group of images is so obvious that its
members are easily ignored: the images contained in play
titles.

The Dance of Death (August Strindberg). How many have worked on this play, yet never bothered to investigate the activity named in the title? By merely looking it up in a dictionary, you can illuminate the entire play and be less puzzled by "enigmatic Strindberg." A dance of death is a medieval dance in which the participants, involved with their lively, intricate movements, do not realize they are being led dance step by dance step to their graves by a skeleton representing death. *The Dance of Death:* the central action of the play is readily apparent in the title—if you've paid attention.

The Glass Menagerie (Tennessee Williams). The image is of a collection of miniature glass animals—delicate, fragile, lifeless—gathering dust. The key to these and other qualities is to simply ask yourself what you associate with the image. The results don't provide rigorous case study, but they do evoke the most important characteristics of the play's people.

The Crucible (Arthur Miller). Possibly you have read *The Crucible*, even acted, directed or designed it, without ever considering its title. "Crucible?" But isn't it a play about witches? Do your own research here, and relate it to the play.

Ghosts (Henrik Ibsen). No one returns from the dead in this play. But still the dead hover over the living. Miss that point and you've missed the play.

A Midsummer Night's Dream. What does the title evoke? Does "midsummer night" make you think of cold and danger, or seriousness and moroseness, or things of great import? Or does it evoke just the opposite? And what about *dreams*? They are things without substance—things not "real"—but we *think* they are very real while they are going on. In this case the title opens the way to the heart of the play.

What *dream* evokes to me is slightly different from what it evokes to you. That is part of its value. The good artist does not seek a group response, but rather a group of individual responses. But images must be chosen that are not likely to evoke a *wrong* response. If Mr. Williams had believed that people think cats like being on hot tin roofs,

he'd have chosen a different title. But he knew our responses would be more or less the same. You and I might
visualize different cats, with different expressions on their
faces, trying different ways to get off the blistering roof, but
even though individualized, the essence of the image holds
from auditor to auditor. *A successful image evokes different
responses from person to person, yet falls within a certain
common range for everyone. Cat on a Hot Tin Roof*, then,
contains a successful image.

Title tells a lot. If you know nothing of seagulls or wild
ducks, find out before reading *The Seagull* or *The Wild Duck*.
Writers sometimes puzzle for days, months, about what to
call a play. The words that compose a title are usually the
most carefully chosen in the script. *If the title contains an
image, know its implications and how they evoke the shape
and/or nature of the play.*

In some households, years ago, at a certain time in the
afternoon or evening all activity came to a stop and attention was turned to the youngsters. Stories were told, games
were played, milk and cookies served. It was the youngsters' time: a good, healthy, and innocent time. Henry
Wadsworth Longfellow wrote about it:

> I hear in the chamber above me
> The patter of little feet,
> The sound of a door that is opened,
> And voices soft and sweet.
>
> From my study I see in the lamplight,
> Descending the broad hall stair,
> Grave Alice, and laughing Allegra,
> And Edith with golden hair.
>
> A whisper, and then a silence:
> Yet I know by their merry eyes
> They are plotting and planning together
> To take me by surprise.

One American playwright, Lillian Hellman, chose the
reaction such a time evokes to create a title of astonishing
irony. Out of that irony comes the power of her play: *The
Children's Hour.*

Don't ignore title. It might be your key to the script:

Endgame, Arsenic and Old Lace, After the Fall, Ashes, A Taste of Honey, The Birthday Party, The Tempest, and on and on and on.

Repeating Images

Images not in the title can be just as important, built to major significance by repetition through the play. *Never underestimate the power of the repeating image.* The moon is not in the title of *A Midsummer Night's Dream* (though "midsummer night" might evoke it), but reference to the moon occurs every few lines from the play's first words to the last. In act 5 a character even impersonates the moon. The moon is always present—but why? What can this image tell us about the action of the play?

With such an extended image the answer is lengthy. But begin with, say, one obvious quality: what is the nature of the moon's light? Is it diffuse and all-illuminating like the sun? Is it warm and comforting like the sun? Is it yellow? No, it is none of these. Lunar light is sharp and milky; it casts strange shadows. It does not reveal true shapes like the sun does, but makes things seem different from what they are by light of day. Moonlight is cold, beautiful and forbidding, enchanting and frightening. It is not like sunlight. It is not yellow. The moon image evokes (by nature of its strange, shape-altering light) illusion, change, indefinite form and nature—and much more.

This scratches the surface of what is evoked by moon imagery: romance, mystery, magic, fear, distance, lunacy—and more still. The more you see of what moon imagery evokes, the more you will understand this play into which the moon is so liberally and intricately woven. Read the play and note every moon reference. Then examine how such references build into a series of rich, evocative elements to which we each, in our individual ways, react.

The dumb reader doesn't notice the moon, so spends most of the play in the dark. The dumb reader's staging of *A Midsummer Night's Dream* is thus dumb theater. *A Midsummer Night's Dream* with no moon is like a day with no sun—or like being lost in the stars without the stars.

Whether major—like *Midsummer*'s moon—or minor ("that writer's ink is grape juice, not wine"), images expand a communication beyond its own confines. Images convey that to which we can react emotionally as well as intellectually; images evoke associations well beyond the factual or conceptual; images provide for personal, individual communication because we each react, in most ways, uniquely. Images are not frills; they are hefty building blocks.

FOCUS: An image is the use of something we know to tell us about something we don't know. "Marvin walks like a camel": what we don't know (how Marvin walks) is described by what we do know (how a camel walks). Images evoke and expand, rather than define and limit. They call up associations that are not precisely the same from audience member to audience member, so provide a particularly personal kind of communication.

12
Theme

. . . this weak and idle theme
No more yielding but a dream.
A Midsummer Night's Dream 5.1.427–28

Ambition, revenge, love, fate, greed, jealousy, parent/child, justice, faith, and so forth—all are abstract concepts. **The *theme* of a play is an abstract concept which part or all of that play is "about."** Many writers are reluctant to discuss *theme*. Ask playwrights what their plays are "about," and they will answer, "About two and a half hours." Theme is an abstraction, but writers are concerned with the concrete. They may be hostile to questions about theme. Countless young readers have been soured on poetry and drama because pedagogues have taught that the purpose of reading a poem or play was to find out what it "meant," as if it were a puzzle or code to be solved, as if poetic or dramatic expression were a communication obstacle to be surmounted. But as Archibald MacLeish—a man who ought to know—states in "Ars Poetica":

A poem should not mean
But be.

Investigation of theme, a poem's or a play's, is *not* an attempt to discover what the work means. A play doesn't *mean* anything. It *is*. Artistic expression is meaning in and of itself. It doesn't translate or decode or puzzle or compute into anything but itself.

Some elements of a play can be abstract topics that

emerge from or are important to the action. One theme of *Hamlet* is revenge. This does not mean that the play's purpose is to study or examine or explore revenge. It only means that revenge is an abstract concept made concrete by the play's action.

Macbeth is not a treatise on ambition. It is a play in which one theme is ambition. Another theme is power, another is guilt. There are more.

King Lear has themes about power, about parent-child relationships, about madness . . . and much, much more. To say that Shakespeare was mainly concerned with any one thins the play of the others.

If a writer has great vision and depth, the play's themes will loom important. If not, theme will not be provender for thought, reflection, and emotional involvement; theme will be merely topic.

In either case, *theme is not what a play means, nor is expression of theme the "purpose" of a play.*

A common and grave error involves delving for theme first and foremost, ignoring other elements of greater and more immediate importance. *King Lear's* themes can't even be considered until the plot is clear. If you don't scrutinize the exposition in the first seven lines you will think scene 1 presents a contest to determine division of the kingdom, and that error will mask the play's true themes for the entire play. (See section 8.)

Theme is a *result*. Look for it *last*. First analyze with care the action, characterization, images, and other components. By then theme will be manifestly apparent almost by itself. If you simply see the motivation that drives Hamlet once the Ghost has told its terrible tale in act 1, scene 5, you cannot miss the revenge theme. It emerges by itself.

Theme cannot be superimposed a priori. If your theater has to take pains to clarify themes for your audience on the lobby walls or the program cover, then you have failed to make the play a working stage piece. There's nothing wrong with little hearts on the program cover for *Love's Labor's Lost,* or handless clocks for *Waiting for Godot,* or white-tipped canes for *Oedipus Tyrannos,* but if you need those things so the audience can figure out what the play's about, you can be sure the components of the work are not all on stage where they belong.

As you do your analytic reading, keep a small list of themes. Some plays have many, though not all are of the same importance. The list will be your guide to abstract concepts the play treats on—but don't get tangled up in them. Don't short-circuit the work of art by ignoring it to get to theme, by busting through the work as if it were a shell, a barrier to be eliminated between audience and play. Theme is conveyed *by* theatricality, not in spite of it.

And don't turn drama into philosophy. There's not an idea in *Hamlet* or *Oedipus Tyrannos* that a moderately bright high school student cannot fully comprehend. Projecting your own (or borrowed) elaborate cogitations onto the profound simplicity of great plays may amuse you but it won't amuse many others.

If you "find" a theme not expressed through action or other major *theatrical* components, it probably isn't genuinely there. Undaunted by nonexistence, some people try to express such themes in their productions. The play is warped by imposition of a theme not inherent in the basic building blocks of drama—blocks which have been the main subject of this book.

Theme can be expressed only by the play's theatrical specifics: action, character, image, and so forth. Hidden subtleties or a reader's outside additions rarely make it past the footlights without interfering with the play. This seems a particularly difficult point for young, enthusiastic directors (and some not so young) who easily fall to the temptation of patching "interesting" themes onto plays with the most scant and subtle evidence.

Theme should emerge from the play. And it will, if you give it the chance. Things won't work the other way round.

FOCUS: A theme is an abstract concept made concrete by a play's action. Theme is not meaning; it is a topic in the play. Theme is a result; it emerges from a script's workings, so examine a play for theme after you are thoroughly familiar with the play's foundation elements.

Part Three

Tricks of the Trade

13
Background Information

Every available kind of information is useful: background information on the author, the era, the artistic environment from which the script emerged, and so on. The most useful information comes from other works by the same author. For example, if you are staging *The Merchant of Venice* and are unfamiliar with other Shakespeare plays you will miss the relationship of Belmont to Venice. Yet the relationship is obvious once you've seen it in several forms in *As You Like It, A Midsummer Night's Dream, The Tempest, Two Gentlemen of Verona*—plays that span the whole of Shakespeare's career.

If you stage John Steinbeck's *Of Mice and Men*, a trap awaits you: making Curly's wife a flirtatious slut (as the bunkhouse guys perceive her). How many unread directors, as insensitive as the bunkhouse guys, have urged equally unread, trusting but uncomfortable, actresses into that trap? Read a few Steinbeck novels and discover the humanity of his perception, for it is central to all his work. Curly's wife is no trouble-making slut slavering for a roll in the hay. She's lonely, looking for company the only way she knows how.

If you are an artist who loves excellence and integrity, read everything your author ever wrote. Go the extra mile.

Leave no stone unturned, for you never know what treasure of understanding lies beneath it. It's a lot of work, and no one holds a gun to your head to do it. But why deliberately aim at mediocrity by saving effort, by being "efficient?"

14
Trusting the Playwright

Assume what's in a script is there on purpose. Assume the writer knew what he or she was doing. If you trust the play enough to stage it, trust its author. If you alter or cut whenever you have difficulty you may miss something important.

A seventy-five line section of *Hamlet* is often cut because it seems irrelevant. But know not "seems." Assume Shakespeare knew what he was up to. The often-cut section directly follows the Ghost's act 1, scene 5 tale of his own murder, and has to do with Polonius' instructions to Reynaldo, who is on his way to spy on Laertes in Paris (2.1).

Many directors too easily give up trying to find the point of this section. Perhaps, because Reynaldo does not appear again in the play, they assume Shakespeare wrote the part for an out-of-work buddy he owed a favor. So the section is omitted from production. The consequences of the omission are grave.

Without that section, Polonius is merely a doddering, harmless old fool. In fact, most readers—failing to see the significance of the Reynaldo section—are certain Polonius *is* a doddering fool. But those seventy-five lines reveal him to be an expert, ruthless spy. He is capable and clever, and though he may babble on now and then, he is a force to be reckoned with and used.

Hamlet eventually kills Polonius. Does he kill a harmless old fool, or a machinating intelligence agent? If the fool, audience reaction to Hamlet will be wrenched out of joint—particularly when Hamlet revels over the killing.

Legitimate reasons to alter or cut a script do exist. But be certain the fault is not in yourself. To convince yourself of the danger of careless cutting, discover the relevance of *spying* in *Hamlet*. Find every instance of spying. Few readers notice, yet spying is one of the play's most common activities. Almost everyone spies—even the Ghost. So think twice before you cut those seventy-five lines. Chances are they have more to do with the play than you do.

15
Families

Customs, styles, politics, laws, tastes, and almost everything else change from age to age, period to period. But something we know intimately changes little: relationships among family members. Anyone who grew up in anything remotely resembling a family might easily understand the human relationships in almost any play simply by taking the trouble to examine the normal, familiar *family* forces involved.

On a most important level, *Hamlet* is about a son, a father, a mother, a girlfriend, an uncle. *King Lear* is about a father and his three daughters, and another father and his two sons. Bring to a play what you know from your own experience with fathers, sons, mothers, daughters, and you can bring home to yourself the play's major dynamics. What you understand about classical Greek ethics and morality is no more useful for a play like *Oedipus Tyrannos* than what you understand about a husband's love for his wife and a son's love for his mother and father.

The same is true for an audience. An audience is more easily able to understand relationships among family members than almost any other kind of human behavior. If *King Lear* is *only* about a king and three princesses it will have little emotional relevance to an audience.

Family relationships are at or near the center of almost every play. Don't ignore this superb means for understanding the play and bringing the audience close to it.

16

Generalities: Mood, Atmosphere

Probably because designers must help create mood, they are often encouraged to read for "atmosphere." Almost nothing could be worse. A play, like life, is composed of specifics. Atmosphere is a generalized *result*, a *consequence* of specifics. Find the specifics and atmosphere will emerge. Start with atmosphere and the specifics will be forever buried.

Spell *mood* backwards.

Four hours of a melancholy *Hamlet* come from reading for mood and atmosphere. No audience wants to be that bored, even for art.

17

The Unique Factor

Playwrights rarely create people living out just another day
in their lives. Something out-of-the-ordinary arises—
usually but not always early in the play—and that causes a
turn from ordinary events, a turn the rest of the play follows.

In *Hamlet* the unique factor is readily apparent: a ghost
arrives that has never arrived before, and that sets off a
series of events that have never happened before. In
Oedipus Tyrannos a plague has now for the first time become unbearable. But *Tartuffe*'s unique factor is not so obvious. It is not the presence of Tartuffe, for he has been in
the household all along. It is something specific Tartuffe
does at this particular time, and you must find what it is.
In *Waiting for Godot* the unique factor is subtle and barely
visible—but it is there. The director who can't find it won't
be able to make act 2 different from act 1.

Sometimes the unique factor is a combination of things,
and sometimes it is a "last straw" effect—something that
has been going on all along but now has finally gone over
the brink.

The unique factor is usually connected to the intrusion
that breaks stasis (see section 4). Sometimes the two are
the same (such as in *Hamlet*) but not always. *King Lear*'s

unique factor is that Lear has never divided his kingdom before—but the intrusion is Cordelia's refusal to say more than "Nothing, my Lord."

The unique factor reveals why the play's events take place on this particular day instead of yesterday or last week or next year. It renders the action of the play specific in time.

One thing that makes real life seem real is the awareness we always have of the specific present moment. Even when engaged in the most mundane of repetitious activities, we usually maintain clear distinction between this moment and all other moments. *Human beings focus on "now."* This same quality of specific *now* must be part of the life portrayed on stage, or that life will seem incomplete, vague, generalized, unreal. Know what makes a play's life specific in time, why the action is unique.

18

Changing Eras

Playwrights—even great ones—do not write for the ages. They write for their specific audiences at their specific times. Some plays prove theatrical to audiences in later periods, but special problems arise when a play is done for an audience other than the one it was written for.

For example, twentieth-century Americans often read *Hamlet* as a play about Elizabethan England with characters (dressed in Elizabethan clothing) behaving as if they are English. But Shakespeare set the play in Denmark, knowing his London audience of 1601 had specific thoughts and feelings about Danes. Modern Americans don't share those thoughts and feelings; they aren't even aware of them.

In 1601 Shakespeare's Londoners had reason to think Denmark a terrifying place, peopled by warlike, bloodthirsty savages. Londoners knew that a few centuries earlier Danes had sailed up the Thames and set fire to London Bridge (hence the nursery rhyme "London Bridge Is Falling Down"). And even in the sixteenth century Danes frequently landed on England's shores to attack isolated villages—killing, raping, and plundering before disappearing back to sea. To Elizabethans, Denmark meant destruction, primitive brutality, and terror.

Into the midst of such a world Shakespeare puts Hamlet.

A major conflict within the play becomes clear: a *man* of introspection and considered thought versus a *society* of impulsive, arbitrary brutality. This conflict partly explains Hamlet's "inability" to act, without resorting to modern psychological theories about melancholia disabling the prince.

It may be coincidence that no one thought Hamlet incapable of action until a hundred years after the play was first staged—right about the same time that the English perception of Denmark as bloody and brutal started disappearing.

For every play from a time and place other than your own, *consider what the original audience thought and felt about the world portrayed in the play.* Sometimes this takes a lot of research, but the results will be worth the effort.

Do not confuse the world in the play (such as Denmark) with the world in which the play was first produced (1601 London). Often there is little in common, and frequently they are opposites. *Oedipus Tyrannos* does not take place in stately, civilized, classical Athens. The play's scenery should not be symmetrical and architecturally pure and balanced, its costumes should not reflect the golden world of fifth century B.C. Greece. *Oedipus Tyrannos* is not set amidst high Attic civilization. Sophocles put the play in Thebes—*much earlier* than the fifth century. Sophocles' Athenian audience regarded early Thebes in a particular way: as a primitive remnant of times long past, not so enlightened as "modern" Athens. This difference between Athens and early Thebes can help illuminate the action of the entire play.

As a result, modern productions may have to go to lengths unnecessary for the original stagings. We may have to help our audiences see what early Thebes was like, whereas Athenians already knew. Here is where good costume and scene design can provide the foundation for sterling production.

Audience reaction to the world in a play usually changes over the ages. Find the change and adjust for it, or you may lose the play altogether. What could more emasculate *Hamlet* than cramming it into a refined English royal court? Shakespeare's production might have been English, because his audience brought with it vibrant awareness of the nature of the Danes. But our audiences don't.

19
Climax

At some point late in a play, the major forces of conflict have at each other. That ultimate fray results in restoration of an equilibrium—either the equilibrium that started the play or a new equilibrium.

Many readers find it useful to see the entire shape of a play as a gradual, step-by-step rise in intensity towards the clash that is the climax, followed by a rapid drop in intensity during final stasis.

20
Beginnings/Endings

The ending of every play (the moments between climax and final curtain) could be the beginning of a new play— because it is a stasis, and stasis begins plays. Similarly, the beginning of every play could be the end of another. It is easy to imagine a play that could have ended in the stasis that begins *Hamlet*. And the end of *Oedipus Tyrannos* is in fact very like the beginning of a play Sophocles wrote years later.

A careful reader will consider what the play might have been that led up to the opening of the play under study. The play following final stasis should be considered too. This helps illuminate the action of the play under study in the larger scope of its world, not merely as an isolated series of events.

21
Rereading

A single reading of a play does not scratch the surface. Now that you are beginning to understand analytic techniques of script reading, you should see that several readings are essential *to begin with*. Never waltz into your first rehearsal or design conference with only a reading or two behind you. That's like learning to drive on ice while already skidding towards a cliff.

The words in a script are intended to be spoken aloud. Before your first rehearsal or conference, read the play out loud to yourself.

22

What Next?

Once you have a detailed, working awareness of a script gained through analytic reading techniques, what do you do?

Take what you have discovered by reading, and use your painstakingly-learned theater crafts and arts to give it to an audience. A designer whose careful reading reveals that *King Lear*'s first scene is no test but rather a public exhibition is ready to think about what the exhibition place looks like and what the exhibitors might wear. An actor doing the Ghost in *Hamlet*'s act 1, scene 5 knows he can severely underplay because both Hamlet and the audience want so desperately to hear that they will provide total attention. A director whose technical analysis reveals that the action of *Oedipus Tyrannos* is launched by a plague will remember that the plague ends once the murderer is discovered. Thereby the director will not miss the point of the play, and—more important—neither will the audience.

If your reading of the script is good enough to reveal the tools, weapons, methods, advantages (and liabilities) provided by the playwright, then (and I swear on my forebears' ghosts, *only* then) are you ready to apply your theater training, your theater arts and crafts, your talent. Any other order of attack robs you of your main ally: the strength of the writer whose script you admire enough to stage.

Think of the script as a tool. Before you pick it up to use, know which is the handle and which is the blade—or you might cut your throat.

Good reading comes first. Read backwards, read forwards. Dumb readers finish last.